Journeying with the Prophets

Written by Serena Husain Yates

Illustrated by Asif Mahmood

Copyright

All rights reserved. No part of this book may be reproduced or transmitted in any form or by any means, electronic, mechanical, including photocopy, recording, or any information storage and retrieval system, without permission in writing from the author.

Contents

The Author	iv
Preface	v
My Legacy	ix

CHAPTER 1   Allah's Creation   1

CHAPTER 2   The Story PF Prophet NUH/NOAH (PBUH)   10

CHAPTER 3   The Story of Prophet HUD   22

CHAPTER 4   The People of Thamud-Prophet - Saleh (AS)   29

CHAPTER 5   The Story of Prophet Shoaib (AS)   35

CHAPTER 6   The Story of Prophet Ibraheem (AS), (Abraham), and Ishmael (AS)   41

CHAPTER 7   The Story of Prophet Ishaaq (AS) and Prophet Yaqub (AS)   48

CHAPTER 8   The Story of Prophet Yusuf (Joseph)   56

CHAPTER 9   The Story of Prophet Musa Alayhi Asalam   66

CHAPTER 10   Prophet Musa and the Bani Israel Settled on the Other Side of the Red Sea.   78

CHAPTER 11   The Story of Prophets Yusha (Joshua) Hizqeel (Ezekiel) Uzair   87

CHAPTER 12   The Story of Prophet Sammil (AS) Samuel, Talut, (Samson), Jalut (Goliath) Prophet Dawood (AS) David   94

CHAPTER 13   The Story of Maryam (Mary) and Prophet ISA (AS) Jesus   101

CHAPTER 14   The Story of Prophet Muhammed (AS)   117

The Author

Written by Serena Husain Yates

Serena Hussain-Yates has been living in the United Kingdom for the last 36 years, having migrated from her native country Guyana.

A mother to four adult children and thirteen grandchildren, the author is the founder of BURTON SISTERS CIRCLE, a dawah giving organisation.

Contact details: serenabibi@aol.com

Illustrated by Asif Mahmood

Contact details: asif.designs@hotmail.com

Preface

Journeying with the prophets is a book that engages the readers to time travel into the lifetime of the prophets, living the life of their people, making their mistakes, receiving their punishments.

The writer aims to spiritually take you there and return you to present day to ponder, evaluate, and self-examine the purpose of your creation.

Death is knocking at every door. There is no discrimination. Coronavirus had caused the world to acknowledge the existence of a higher intelligent being, a creator, one who is almighty. God in a short pace of time has changed the whole dynamics of the world.

This universe is created in perfect harmony and balance. The earth's distance from the sun, the thickness of the earth's crust, the speed at which the earth revolves, the percentage of oxygen in the atmosphere, and even the earth's tilt. If these measurements were slightly different to what they currently are, life could not exist.

Our creator did not leave us here to wander blindly. In every nation he sends Prophets and messengers. As it is not possible for human beings to have a detailed knowledge of God except through revelation from Himself, God sent His Messengers to teach the people about their Creator, who they must worship. These Messengers also brought with them the details of how to worship God, because such details cannot be known except by way of revelation. These two fundamentals were the most important things that the Messengers of all the divine revelations brought with them from God. On this basis, all the divine revelations have had the same lofty objectives, which are:

To worship one God and to follow all of God's rules to exist in peace and harmony in his world.

Each nation had its own messengers but Prophet Mohammed (PBUH) was sent to guide all mankind.

God has revealed the stories of previous peoples for a specific reason; so that by learning about, reflecting upon, and understanding their stories we take lessons which will help us in our own lives. Thus, learning about them is not idle talk or a waste of time.

The experiences of the people of the past can teach us a lot about life, about ourselves, and about God's plan for His servants and the wisdoms behind it. From the first "story" of our father Adam (peace be upon him) we find the "story" of humanity. It is the story of God's servant who forgets his Lord and falls into error. This is the human condition in a nutshell. But more importantly his story teaches us the other part of the human experience, which is repentance. How do we correct our errors? How can God forgive us after we abandoned His message, and after we have followed our own desires instead of what God wants from us?

Thus, God is telling us that what happened to them can most assuredly happen to us if we're not on guard. He is also warning us that our fall might be final as well. Although Adam was blessed to be able to repent to God and have his repentance accepted, we are not guaranteed the same fate. While we believe in God's ultimate mercy toward the believers, we know that it is possible that He will hold us to account for our sins. This punishment could be given in this world or in the next life, which only God knows the severity of. He says, "Inform My servants that I am the Forgiver, the Merciful, but that My punishment is a painful punishment" (15:49-50). Because of this truth, the believer must strive to live their lives free from sins, and to hold themselves accountable for their mistakes when they occur; seeking God's forgiveness and guidance in all their affairs.

Journeying with the Prophets takes you through the era of Prophets Adam, Noah, Hud, Saleh, Shoaib, Abraham, Isaacs, Ismail, Jacob, Joseph, Moses, Joshua, Ezekiel, Ezra, Samuel, David, John, Zacharia, John, Mary and Jesus, John, and the seal of all Prophets Muhammed (May the peace and blessings of God be upon them all).

These stories must not be read for entertainment or just for bedtime, but for solace to face the world's trials and tribulations.

QURAN

The Quran is the divine scripture or sacred text of the religion of Islam. Muslims believe that the Quran is the literal word of God. The Quran is the last testament in a series of divine revelations from God (*Allah* in Arabic). It consists of the unaltered and direct words of God, which were revealed through the Angel Gabriel to Muhammad, the final prophet of Islam, more than 1400 years ago. Quran confirms the books that were sent before it, including the Jewish Torah and the Gospels of Jesus. It became the book of guidance for all humankind. Quran abrogates all scriptures before it.

It contains signs of God's greatness, miracles, parables, and lessons. The Quran explains the names and attributes of God and His creations. It calls us to believe in God, His angels, His Books, His Messengers, the Last Day, and in in fate or the divine decree.

Islam is a continuation of the message received by previous prophets, such as Noah, Abraham, David, Moses and Jesus, peace be upon them all. Therefore, the Quran maintains the pure teachings of previous revelations, including the Torah and the Gospel. The Quran describes that all the prophets taught people to believe in the One God, the Creator. The messengers also instructed them to spend their lives with God-consciousness, doing good deeds and avoiding sins. Moreover, they warned their fellow humans of accountability in the afterlife, a subject which the Quran returns to again and again.

WHY ISLAM

For those who do not believe in a creator, are you going to wait until you die to find out. Put it this way – if you heard that the Covid-19 had re-occur in China, but you are not sure, will you visit without taking all the necessary precautions? If there isn't then at least you have prepared. It's a win win situation.

It's the same in the belief in the hereafter. Are you going to wait until you are there??? With present day, it might be sooner than later.

So, you have explored other religions and you perceive shortcomings and you are looking for answers elsewhere. Try exploring Islam.

The core belief of Islam is that there is a God who created us. He is fair and just, and He wants us to achieve the reward of paradise. However, God has placed us in this journey of life as a test. But if we are left to our own devices, we will be lost because we don't know what He wants from us. We cannot make this journey without His guidance. God sent messengers to give us this guidance. If the previous scriptures are corrupt, how will you know that the Islamic scripture isnt?

The answer in a nutshell. God has stopped sending messengers and revelations because he tells us that Prophet Muhammed will be the last and final messenger and the Quran will be preserved.

The Quran was revealed over a period of twenty-three years and was written down in its entirety during the Prophet's lifetime. In every generation they are those who memorise it. It's the same Quran everywhere. There is no variation. If all the Quran were to be destroyed, then the message will still be intact as it has been memorised.

Why Islam??

Because Islam provides a clear understanding of a person's relationship with God, purpose in life, and ultimate destiny.

My Legacy

My children,

My grandchildren,

I leave this book as a legacy to you. In this journey of life Allah has chosen me to be your guardian, your protector. Allah has entrusted me, gifted me with the best of treasures, my beautiful family.

Live your life in the submission and affirmation to the one God.

All that exists belongs to Him as He is the Originator of all. He, subhanahu, alone is worthy of worship and all other deities are to be shunned.

Everything happens by the Qader (will) of subhanahu. What was never meant for you will never reach you and what is meant for you, you will never have missed.

Live your life with kindness, gratitude. Live everyday as the last day of your life. Seek refuge in Allah from the accursed Shaitan who lies waiting to trap you.

Fulfil your duties to one another. You might be four different families but live your life as one. There is nothing greater than kinship.

Remember that happiness comes with a pure heart free from jealousy, hatred, arrogance.

Establish your prayers regularly and with humility. Nothing in your life is more important than your Salaat. Prayer is your connection to Allah.

Feel the hunger and thirst of others. Thank Allah in all conditions. He may know a thing that's good for and that what is bad.

Learn the lessons from the Prophets. Put your trust in Allah and avoid those who aim to cause mischief. Speak well of others and avoid slander and backbiting.

Live your life with contentment and avoid excess. Have pleasure in giving than receiving.

Be charitable to your neighbours and love for yourself what you love for your brother. Live your life with tolerance and be accepting of others, even if their beliefs differ from you.

Ask forgiveness from those you harm and repent to Allah.

I pray that Allah protect and guide each and everyone one of you and we meet again and live as one family in Jannatul Firdous.

AMEEN

Mummy, Nani Serena.

x ■ Serena Husain Yates

CHAPTER 1

Allah's Creation

It's been a very exciting time for Layla and her siblings. In fact, the excitement is oozing out of all the Yates children. Yes!!! All thirteen of them.

It was the time of the Covid-19 virus. Layla couldn't understand why all the adults are so sad. The kids are having such a wonderful time. Everyone is being home schooled. Hooray!

Every day the children are doing such exciting things. The mummies and daddies are staying home. The children are enjoying the sleeping ins. They plan the day together and do things that they want to do and that's why they feel that they are gaining so much knowledge. Staying at home is so much better than going to school.

They all cook their meals together, dine together, read salah and Quran together.

They felt that it was the best times of their lives.

But today is going to be extra special. All thirteen of the children are going to Nani's Serena's house. You see Nani Serena is not only an excellent storyteller but also a good cook and always have a good supply of treats.

When Layla and her brothers Musa and Aaron arrived, the other cousins were already there. They were all sitting some distance from each other.

"Don't give hugs and kisses kids", Nani Serena reminded. But all the children already knew what to do to stop the virus from spreading.

"Asalam Alaikum"

Layla and her brothers greeted Nani Serena and the ten cousins. Its always a happy time when all the cousins meet up.

"Walaikum Asalam"

Responded Keyaan, Leyah, Jasmine, Tariq, Eva, Amelia, Omari, Siyana, Zayn and Seth.

People are getting sick, people are dying. Everyone is saying to have faith in Allah. The grandchildren posed so many questions to Nani Serena.

Who is Allah?

Who made us?

Why are we here?

What happens to us when we die?

"Okay children, Nani Serena replied with great enthusiasm, "I will tell you a very long story. I will start right from the beginning.

Children, I now want you to think back how it was when there was nothing on this earth. Can you imagine that?

"Kids, I have a great idea", shouted Keyaan excitedly. We can close our eyes and think hard. So, all the children closed their eyes. Nani gave them a few minutes and then told them to open their eyes.

They were all very eager to discuss their imagination. They share their thoughts of this journey they had just went on.

Leyah summarised all the children's notions when she said:

"Yes Nani I went back in time. It was so strange. There were no trees, no animals, no mountains, no rivers and NO PEOPLE."

Musa then put his very serious, pensive face on and asked:

"Well, where was everyone?"

So Nani Serena began her story.

In the beginning there was just Allah. He sat on his throne, which was above water.

Allah then created the heaven and the earth and told the pen which he created, to write everything that will happen on earth until the end of the world.

"And where is that Book now Nani", curiously asked Jasmine.

Nani Serena informed everyone that special book is kept in heaven.

"And when did God created us" Aaron asked?

"What about the Angels and Jinns" Eva and Tariq added?

Nani Serena was very happy with all the questions the children were asking.

Allah created the angels from light and the Jinns from fire. The Jinns live on earth and the angels live in heaven.

The Angels can only do what Allah commands them to do. But the Jinns can choose between right and wrong.

The Jinns and the Angels are invisible. That means we cannot see them.

Nani Serena was then interrupted by a very worried Omari.

"Nani, you haven't old us who Allah is".

"Okay", Omari, Nani Serena said calmly. Let me tell you who Allah is and then I will continue with the story of how Allah created the first human.

Allah is the one who created everything. Allah loves us more than our mummies and daddies. Allah hasn't got a mummy or daddy or a wife and no children. We are all Allah's children.

Allah does not sleep, and he hears and knows everything. He doesn't even need food. Allah is not like us. Allah can do everything.

Now children, who can remember Allah's other creations?

All hands went up.

"Yes Amelia, you tell us" said Nani Serena

"Jinns", said Amelia gleefully!!

"And Siyana, what will you like to say"?

"Angels nani, replied Siyana.

Nani Serena told the children about a special Jinn who was living in the heavens with Allah and the Angels. He was a good Jinn and so Allah called him to live in the heavens.

And who can tell me what Allah created the Jinns from.

Up goes Zayn's hand.

"Allah made the Jinns from fire" Zayn told everyone.

Seth was looking rather sad by now.

"Why are you sad Seth", asked Nani Serena sympathetically.

Before Seth could even answer, his siblings Layla, Musa and Aaron sternly told Nani Serena that he didn't answer any questions.

"Oh, but I am not finished with my questions yet", Nani Serena said with a twinkle in her eyes.

"Ok Seth. What are the Angels made off?"

"Light!!! Light". Seth was so pleased with his answer. Nani and all the children praised him. You see Seth is the youngest of Nani Serena's grandkids. Seth is the baby of the Yates Family. And all the children are very fond of him.

ALLAH CREATED ADAM (PBUH)

The children now settled down and Nani has their sole attention as she tells the story of Adam.

Adam was not only the first man Allah created but he was also the first prophet. He was neither created from light or fire, but from soil.

Allah told the angels to gather soil from different parts of the world. This he used with water to create the Adam. He was then shaped into a human form and remained in that state for forty years.

"You remember that good Jinn that was living in heaven with the Angels?", Nani Serena tested the children.

All the children remembered him.

Nani explained how that good Jinn used to walk around Adam. He was very curious of this creation.

He wasn't happy that Allah made another being.

Then one day Allah blew life into Adam. Allah gave him a soul. He came alive. So, Allah told all the Angels and that Jinn to bow down to him. The Angels did but not that Jinn. He disobeyed Allah. He said that he was better than Adam because he was made from soil and him, the jinn, was made from fire.

Allah was very angry with him and told him that he will send him to hell.

On that day he became a Shaitan and his name is now Iblis. He asked if Allah could let him live until the world ends. He also requested Allah to give him special powers to take Adam and his children with him to the hellfire.

"Nani, said Keyaan, "I need to ask you an important question. I want to know when we were created".

Nani answered Keyaan's question by explaining that the souls of everyone who has lived and who will live on earth was created and placed in the backbone of Adam. Allah introduced himself to us then but then wiped out that memory. Allah tells us this in Surah Al Araf.

He said he will come from all directions to make the children of Adam disobey Allah's rules so that he can take them to the hellfire.

In deep thought with his finger on his cheeks Musa said:

"Hang on, we are the children of Adam, aren't we? Is he going to take us to the hellfire if we disobeyed Allah's rules?".

Keyaan with an extremely worried expression blurted out loudly:

"Now I know why all the adults are worried about the virus. Those who haven't followed Allah's rules will be thrown into the hellfire".

Now all the children seemed very worried.

Nani Serena told the children that so long as everyone worship Allah they will be safe.

THE CHILDREN OF ADAM AND HAWA

Then Allah created Hawa because Adam will be very lonely on his own. So, now we have Adam and Hawa who are living in Paradise. Allah told them that they can eat the fruits from all the trees except from one tree.

Remember how Shaitaan wants to take Adam and his children to the hellfire if they disobey Allah?

Well Shaitaan although not living in paradise whispered to them to eat the fruits from that tree. They forgot what Allah had told them and ate the fruits.

All the children gasped.

Everything changed that day.

Now you must be thinking that now Adam and Hawa will have to go to the hellfire.

That's wrong.

They were so sorry for what they had done and begged Allah for forgiveness. Allah forgave them but like Shaitaan they also had to leave paradise.

So now we have Adam, Hawa and Shaitaan and all the jinns living on earth.

As the years go by Hawa gave birth to a set of twins. A boy and a girl.

Then another set of twins were born. One boy and one girl.

They name the boys Habeel and Kabeel.

When Habeel and Kabeel became adults, Allah instructed them to get married. Since there were no other females on earth Habeel was instructed to marry Kabeel's twin sister and Kabeel to marry Habeel's twin sister.

Habeel was very pious and was in total agreement, but Kabeel disobeyed Allah declaring that he wanted to marry his own twin.

Adam decided to settle the matter by telling the boys to make a sacrifice, and the one whose sacrifice is accepted will have his wishes granted.

Habeel, who was a shepherd selected his best lamb for the sacrifice whilst Kabeel, a farmer offered his worst crops.

Allah accepted Habeel sacrifice

Arrogance and envy became the downfall of Kabeel. He killed his brother and then later buried him.

"Nani, nani", said Layla. How did he know how to bury Habeel?

Nani Serena was very pleased with the question and proceed to give her answer.

Nani Serena explained that Kabeel carried his dead brother on his shoulders for days because he didn't know what to do with his body. Allah then sent two ravens. These two ravens started fighting. One raven killed the other, scratched the ground with its feet and buried the dead one. When Kabeel saw what the raven did he dug the earth and buried his brother.

Adam and Hawa went on to have many children. Except for one child they were all twins.

Nani Serena looked straight at Seth and asked him if he knew the name of that special child who wasn't a twin.

He shook his head.

"His name was Seth, like you!!. Allah gave Adam and Hawa Seth as a gift because Kabeel murdered Habeel.

"Am I a gift to my mummy and daddy" exclaimed Seth.

All the children agreed he was.

When Adam was 960 years old, Allah sent the Angel of death to take his life.

Before Adam died, he reminded all the children that there is only one God and they must only worship that one God. He told them that Allah, who is God, will send many prophets to teach all his children how to live their on earth by following his decree. He also reminded them of Shaitaan.

After the death of Adam, Seth became his successor.

As time goes by, the population on earth grew.

The descendants of Kabeel lived in the valleys and all the other descendants of Adam lived on the mountains.

They lived peacefully in submission to Allah.

Shaitaan was most displeased.

"Who can tell me why"?

All hands went up.

"I will like to" said Layla. "Because he hasn't got anyone to take to the hellfire with him".

"That's correct Layla", said Nani Serena.

So Shaitaan started to put a plan in action. He went to the descendants of Kabeel in the valley and lived amongst them. He pretended to be a nice young boy. He approached a blacksmith and asked if he could work with him. When the blacksmith agreed he started to put his plan in action.

Shaitaan made musical instruments and gave it to the descendants of Kabeel. So, every night everyone would gather and make music with these instruments.

From the music, came the dancing.

Curiosity got the better of the others who lived on the mountains, and eventually they joined their cousins. It was like what we now called street parties.

From the street parties came the immoral behaviour. Allah tells us that there is a shaitaan waiting at every path to lead us astray.

In this instance, he started with just providing the musical instruments and gradually this led to immorality.

At this point Layla, at nine years old is the oldest of Nani Serena's grandchildren, stood up.

"I would like to say something. School discos. This could also lead to immorality. So, it's better to avoid".

Nani Serena was extremely pleased that Layla made this point.

It has been a long day and its time for the children to have their meal and treats.

After washing their hands, they all sat on their cushions, quite apart from each other. They did this because they did not want to catch the virus.

Leyah reminded all the children to say Bismilliah before eating.

"If you don't say bismillah, then the shaitaan will eat with you".

All the children said "Bismilliah" and enjoyed their chowmein and chocolate cake.

The day has now come to an end and its time to go home to their mummies and daddies.

"Thank you children and see you on Tuesday when I will tell you the story of Prophet Nuh", Nani Serena said as she waved goodbye.

SOURCES OF INFORMATION

Creation of the Universe

It is He who created for you all of that which is on the earth. Then He directed Himself to the heaven, [His being above all creation], and made them seven heavens, and He is Knowing of all things. (Al Baqarah verse 29)

A revelation from He who created the earth and highest heavens (Ta-Ha verse 4)

Indeed, your Lord is Allah, who created the heavens and earth in six days and then established Himself above the Throne. He covers the night with the day, [another night] chasing it rapidly; and [He created] the sun, the moon, and the stars, subjected by His command. Unquestionably, His is the creation and the command; blessed is Allah, Lord of the worlds. (Al Araf verse 54)

Indeed, your Lord is Allah, who created the heavens and the earth in six days and then established Himself above the Throne, arranging the matter [of His creation]. There is no intercessor except after His permission. That is Allah, your Lord, so worship Him. Then will you not remember? (Yunus verse 3)

And it is He who created the heavens and the earth in six days - and His Throne had been upon water - that He might test you as to which of you is best in deed. But if you say, "Indeed, you are resurrected after death," those who disbelieve will surely say, "This is not but obvious magic." (Hud, verse 7)

He who created the heavens and the earth and what is between them in six days and then established Himself above the Throne - the Most Merciful, so ask about Him one well informed. (A-Furqan verse 59);

CHAPTER 2

The Story PF Prophet NUH/NOAH (PBUH)

The day has come.

Wednesday is here.

Nani Serena had promised to tell the children the Story of Noah.

But Allah is the best of Planners.

That's why we must always say "Inshaallah" before we say we will do anything. Inshallah means only if Allah permits it.

And Allah did not permit that all the children should meet up again.

The children are not allowed to leave the house. The situation with the Corona Virus is getting worse and everyone is advised to go out only when it is necessary.

Nani Serena had a very long, hard think of this situation and decided that she will visit the grandchildren. She will use Facetime so that all the other grandchildren can join in virtually.

Nani Serena is not breaking the rule of the country because she will be travelling to teach the children. And that's allowed.

Today she will be visiting Jasmine, Tariq and Amelia.

When Nani Serena arrived, the children were already seated on the sofa. Because they are all siblings and in their own homes, they can do this.

"As promised children, today I will tell you the story of Noah", Nani Serena reminded them.

"Jasmine, do you remember our last story", Nani Serena asked Jasmine.

Jasmine was beaming and was so excited to retell.

So, Jasmine started her summary:

"We learnt who Allah is.

Allah can do all things and Allah created everything on earth, the heavens and the universe and everything between them.

We learnt about Shaitaan, Angels and how Allah created Prophet Adam, about his life and his children.

We also learnt how Shaitaan can trick us into breaking Allah's rules so he can take us to the hellfire.

We know now that going to the school disco is breaking Allah's rules.

"Well done, masallah Jasmine", Nani Serena praised five

year old Jasmine.

Nani now started to tell the story of Prophet Noah.

A thousand years after Prophet Adam lived the world had changed. Before He died, Prophet Adam told the people to worship just one God, because there is only one God. Adam also said that Allah will send many prophets to help the people to follow his rules.

So now a thousand years later the people became very bad. They are breaking all of Allah's laws. Instead of worshipping Allah, they started worshipping idols.

"So Shaitaan will be very happy then", Tariq said in a relaxed manner. "They can all join Shaitaan in the hellfire."

Nani Serena corrected him and explained that Allah is full of mercy and do not want the children of Adam to go to the hellfire without sending his prophets to remind them of his rules. Only if they continue disobeying the prophets then they will be sent to the hellfire.

Hence, Allah sent Prophet Noah to guide the people.

Prophet Noah explained to the people that they must not worship the idols. They must only worship Allah.

Only some poor people listened, and the rest continued to worship the idols breaking Allah's rules.

But the prophet was very patient and spoke so well to the people telling them that it was Allah who created everything and we must only worship him.

He reminded them that Allah created this world with everything in it just for us and they must not worship idols.

Amelia looked very puzzled and blurted:

"How can the idols do anything. They can't even move, speak, walk, eat. And Allah has created this entire world for us. Those people are bad people. They deserve to be with Shaitaan in the hellfire if they do not listen to Prophet Noah".

"Yes. That's what I was saying all along" said Tariq in his usual relaxed manner.

"If they do not follow Allah's rule and don't listen to Prophet Noah then they deserve to be in the hellfire."

Nani Serena agreed.

The patient Prophet Noah continued to tell the bad people to follow Allah's rules but instead of listening they started hurting the prophet. They throw stones at him and beat him with a stick.

Prophet Noah continued to call out to the people and tell them that Allah will punish them one day. But still the people did not listen.

He continued preaching to them for 950 years but still the bad people did not listen.

Prophet Noah was very sad.

Allah spoke to the prophet one night, telling him not to be sad and that he will punish all the bad people.

Nani Serena paused and gave the children the opportunity for them to express their thoughts.

"Allah is so merciful and Prophet Noah is so patient", said Jasmine sadly. Allah gave them so many chances and they did not listen."

Tariq with a smirk on his face spoke:

"Well Shaitaan is surely winning. That's why I like to learn about Allah's laws to follow them. The Shaitaan will not take me because I will always be good and worship only Allah".

"Me too, Tariq", said Amelia.

Allah has a greater plan for the wicked people. He asked Prophet Noah and the good people to plant many trees.

Although he did not understand why Allah asked him to do this, he knows that Allah is all wise.

He and the good people started planting the trees.

They planted the trees for more than one hundred years. It was a different time then and the people lived for many hundred years before they die.

When Allah spoke to prophet Noah next, he told him to cut all the trees down and to build a ship. The ship will have to be very, very, big ship.

All the good people helped Prophet Noah to build the ship. They started building by the mountains, far away from the city.

They worked very hard to build this ship.

When the bad people saw what they were doing they made so much fun of them.

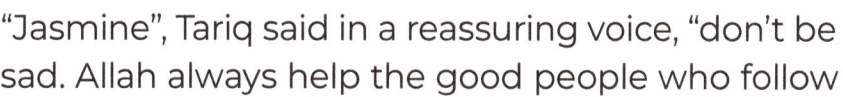

"Well, that's a very unkind thing to do", said Jasmine. "That's bullying".

"Jasmine", Tariq said in a reassuring voice, "don't be sad. Allah always help the good people who follow his rules. Allah will help them and remember the bad people will have to join Shaitaan in the hellfire."

Amelia nodded in agreement.

Finally, they finished building the ship. The good people then prayed to Allah, thanking him as they have completed this job.

This large ship had three different sections.

The first part is for the birds, the second part is for the humans and the third part for the animals.

Allah told Prophet Noah that there will be a flood and that will happen when he sees water coming out of his stove.

As the days of the flood started getting closer Prophet Noah and the good people started leading the animals into the ship. They arrive two by two, in pairs. One male and one female.

Now all the animals and birds were in the ship.

Then it happened. As Allah promised the prophet saw water coming out of the stove in his kitchen.

THE TIME OF THE FLOOD HAS ARRIVED

The rain started falling heavily.

Prophet Noah rushed out and call out to the good people to get into the ship.

Yet, even now the bad people were still laughing at the good people when they were entering the ship.

Even one of his wives and son refused to enter the ship.

Everywhere flooded as the rain began falling heavily.

Only now the people realised that the prophet was speaking the truth.

They started running very fast to the mountains thinking that the water will not reach them there.

He once again called out to his wife and son to join him, but they ignored him thinking that the water will not reach them.

But then the water covered the mountain tops and all the bad people died.

Prophet Noah's ship started moving as soon as he said Bismilliah.

"Did all the bad people really die"? Amelia said meekly.

Tariq responded:

"Yes, they did Amelia. Instead of following Allah they follow the Shaitaan".

"And they will be in the hellfire with Shaitaan", added Jasmine.

The ship sailed for a very long time.

There were 80 people in it and lots of animals.

They had a lockdown like us.

But we have to thank Allah because our lockdown is easy. We have plentiful of everything and we are not locked up in a ship. We are all in our own houses with our families.

Finally, land was in sight. It was Mount Judi in the South East of Turkey.

The Prophet said "Bismillah" and the ship stopped.

The next story will be THE PROPHET HUD AND THE PEOPLE OF AAD.

Nani Serena will be visiting another of her family to tell that story.

SOURCES OF INFORMATION

Prophet NUH (PBUH)

Certainly We sent Nuh to his people, so he said: O my people! serve Allah, you have no god other than Him; surely I fear for you the chastisement of a grievous day. Al-A'raf verne 59

The chiefs of his people said: Most surely we see you in clear error. Al-A'raf verse 60

He said: O my people! There is no error in me, but I am an messenger from the Lord of the worlds. Al-A'raf verne 61

I deliver to you the messages of my Lord, and I offer you good advice and I know from Allah what you do not know. Al-A'raf verne 52

What! do you wonder that a reminder has come to you from your Lord through a man from among you, that he might warn you and that you might guard (against evill and so that mercy may be shown to you? Al-A'raf verne 63

But they called him a liar, so We delivered him and those with him in the ark, and We drowned those who rejected Our communications; surely they were a blind people. Al-A'raf verne 64

And recite to them the story of Nuh when he said to his people: O my people! if my stay and my reminding (you) by the communications of Allah is hard on you, yet on Allah do I rely, then resolve upon your affair and (gather) your associates, then let not your affair remain dubious to you, then have it executed against me and give me no respite: (Yunis verse 71)

But if you turn back, I did not ask for any reward from you; my reward is only with Allah, and I am commanded that I should be of those who submit. (Yunis verne 72)

But they rejected him, so We delivered him and those with him in the ark, and We made them rulers and drowned those who rejected Our communications; see then what was the end of the (people) warned. (Yunis verse 73)

Journeying with the Prophets

And certainly We sent Nuh to his people: Surely I am a plain warner for you. (Hud verne 25)

That you shall not serve any but Allah, surely I fear for you the punishment of a painful day. (Hud verne 25)

But the chiefs of those who disbelieved from among his people said: We do not consider you but a mortal like ourselves, and we do not see any have followed you but those who are the meanest of us at first thought and we do not see in you any excellence over us; nay, we deem you liars... (Hud verse 27)

He said: O my people! tell me if I have with me clear proof from my Lord, and He has granted me mercy from Himself and it has been made obscure to you; shall we constrain you to (accept) it while you are averse from it? . (Hud verne 28)

And, O my people! I ask you not for weakh in return for it; my reward is only with Allah and I am not going to drive away those who believe; surely they shall meet their Lord, but I consider you a people who are ignorant: . (Hud verse 29)

And, O my people! Who will help me against Allah if I drive them away? Will you not then mind? (Hud verse 30)

And I do not say to you that I have the treasures of Allah and I do not know the unseen, nor do I say that I am an angel, nor do I say about those whom your eyes hold in mean estimation (that) Allah will never grant them (any) good, Allah knows best what is in their souls, for then most surely I should be of the unjust .. (Hud verne 31)

They said: O Nuh! Indeed you have disputed with us and lengthened dispute with us, therefore bring to us what you threaten us with, if you are of the truthful ones. (Hud verne 32)

He said: Allah only will bring it to you if He please, and you will not escape: . (Hud verse 33)

And if I intend to give you good advice, my advice will not profit you if Allah intended that He should leave you to go astray; He is your Lord, and to Him shall you be returned... (Hud verne 34)

Or do they say: He has forged it? Say: If I have forged it, on me is my guilt, and I am clear of that of which you are guilty .. (Hud verse 35)

And it was revealed to Nuh: That none of your people will believe except those who have already believed, therefore do not grieve at what they do: . (Hud verse 36)

And make the ark before Our eyes and (according to) Our revelation, and do not speak to Me in respect of those who are unjust; surely they shall be drowned… (Hud verse 37)

And he began to make the ark; and whenever the chiefs from among his people passed by him they laughed at him. He said: If you laugh at us, surely we too laugh at you as you laugh (at us)… (Hud verse 38)

So shall you know who it is on whom will come a chastisement which will disgrace him, and on whom will lasting chastisement come down. (Hud verse 39)

Until when Our command came and water came forth from the valley, We said: Carry in it two of all things, a pair, and your own family, except those against whom the word has already gone forth, and those who believe. And there believed not with him but a few. (Hud verse 40)

And he said: Embark in it, in the name of Allah be its sailing and its anchoring; most surely my Lord is Forgiving, Merciful. (Hud verse 41)

And it moved on with them amid waves like mountains; and Nuh called out to his son, and he was aloof: O my son! Embark with us and be not with the unbelievers. (Hud verse 42)

He said: I will betake myself for refuge to a mountain that shall protect me from the water. Nuh said: There is no protector today from Allah's punishment but He Who has mercy; and a wave intervened between them, so he was of the drowned. (Hud verse 43)

And it was said: O earth, swallow down your water, and O cloud, clear away; and the water was made to abate and the affair was decided, and the ark rested on the Judi, and it was said: Away with the unjust people. (Hud verse 44)

Journeying with the Prophets

And Nuh cried out to his Lord and said: My Lord! Surely my son is of my family, and Thy promise is surely true, and Thou art the most just of the judges. (Hud verse 45)

He said: O Nuh! Surely he is not of your family; surely he is (the doer of) other than good deeds, therefore ask not of Me that of which you have no knowledge; surely I admonish you lest you may be of the ignorant (Hud verse 46)

He said: My Lord! I seek refuge in Thee from asking Thee that of which I have no knowledge; and if Thou shouldst not forgive me and have mercy on me, I should be of the losers. (Hud verse 47)

[11:48]It was said: O Nuh! Descend with peace from Us and blessings on you and on the people from among those who are with you, and there shall be nations whom We will afford provisions, then a painful punishment from Us shall afflict them. (Hud verse 48)

And Nuh, when he cried aforetime, so We answered him, and delivered him and his followers from the great calamity. (AL-Anbya verse 76)

And We helped him against the people who rejected Our communications; surely they were an evil people, so We drowned them all. (Al-Anbya verse 77)

And certainly We sent Nuh to his people, and he said: O my people! Serve Allah, you have no god other than Him; will you not then guard (against evil? (Al-Muminun verse 23)

And the chiefs of those who disbelieved from among his people said: He is nothing but a mortal like yourselves who desires that he may have superiority over you, and if Allah had pleased, He could certainly have sent down angels. We have not heard of this among our fathers of yore: (Al-Muminun verse 24)

He is only a madman, so bear with him for a time. (Al-Muminun verse 25)

He said: O my Lord! Help me against their calling me a liar. (Al-Muminun verse 26)

So We revealed to him, saying: Make the ark before Our eyes and (according to) Our revelation; and when Our command is given and the valley overflows, take into it of every kind a pair, two, and your followers, except those among them against whom the word has gone forth, and do not speak to Me in respect of those who are unjust; surely they shall be drowned. (Al-Muminun verse 27)

And when you are firmly seated, you and those with you, in the ark, say: All praise is due to Allah who delivered us from the unjust people: (Al-Muminun verse 28)

And say: O my Lord! Cause me to disembark a blessed alighting, and Thou art the best to cause to alight. (Al-Muminun verse 29)

Most surely there are signs in this, and most surely We are ever trying (men). (Al-Muminun verse 30)

And the people of Nuh, when they rejected the messengers, We drowned them, and made them a sign for men, and We have prepared a painful punishment for the unjust; (Al-Furqan verse 27)

The people of Nuh rejected the messengers. (As Ash'ura verse 105)

When their brother Nuh said to them: Will you not guard (against evil? (As Ash'ura verse 106)

Surely I am a faithful messenger to you; (As Ash'ura verse 107)

Therefore guard against (the punishment of) Allah and obey me (As Ash'ura verse 108)

And I do not ask you any reward for it; my reward is only with the Lord of the worlds: (As Ash'ura verse 109)

So guard against (the punishment of) Allah and obey me. (A Ah'ura verse 110)

They said: Shall we believe in you while the meanest follow you? (A Ah'ura verse 111)

He said: And what knowledge have I of what they do? (A Ah'ura verse 112)

Their account is only with my Lord, if you could perceive (A Ah'ura verse 113)

Journeying with the Prophets

And I am not going to drive away the believers; (A Ah'ura verse 114)

I am naught but a plain warner. (A Ah'ura verse 115)

They said: If you desist not, O Nuh, you shall most certainly be of those stoned to death. (A Ah'ura verse 105)

He said: My Lord! Surely my people give me the lie! (A Ah'ura verse 117)

Therefore judge Thou between me and them with a (just) judgment, and deliver me and those who are with me of the believers. (A Ah'ura verse 118)

So We delivered him and those with him in the laden ark. (A Ah'ura verse 119)

Then We drowned the rest afterwards (A Ah'ura verse 120)

Most surely there is a sign in this, but most of them do not believe. (A Ah'ura verse 121)

And most surely your Lord is the Mighty, the Merciful. (A Ah'ura verse 122)

And certainly We sent Nuh to his people, so he remained among them a thousand years save fifty years . And the deluge overtook them, while they were unjust. (Al Ankabut verse 14)

So We delivered him and the inmates of the ark, and made it a sign to the nations. (Al Ankabut verse 15)

And Nuh did certainly call upon Us, and most excellent answerer of prayer are We. (Al verse 14)

And We delivered him and his followers from the mighty distress. (As-Saffat verse 76)

And We made his offspring the survivors.. (As-Saffat verse 77)

And We perpetuated to him (praise) among the later generations.. (As-Saffat verse 78)

Peace and salutation to Nuh among the nations.. (As-Saffat verse 79)

*Thus do We surely reward the doers of good.. (As-Saffat verse 80)
Surely he was of Our believing servants.. (As-Saffat verse 81)*

Then We drowned the others. (As-Saffat verse 82)

And (we destroyed) the people of Nuh before, surely they were a transgressing people.

Before them the people of Nuh rejected, so they rejected Our servant and called (him) mad, and he was driven away.. (Al Qamar verse 9)

Therefore he called upon his Lord: I am overcome, come Thou then to help.. (Al Qamar verse 10)

So We opened the gates of the cloud with water pouring. (Al Qamar verse 11)

And We made water to flow forth in the land in springs, so the water gathered together according to a measure already ordained.. (Al Qamar verse 12)

And We bore him on that which was made of planks and nails. (Al Qamar verse 13)

Sailing, before Our eyes, a reward for him who was denied.. (Al Qamar verse 14)

And certainly We left it as a sign, but is there anyone who remembers? (Al Qamar verse 15)

Journeying with the Prophets

CHAPTER 3
The Story of Prophet HUD

Nani Serena has decided that today she will visit the Arshad family. All the other grandchildren will be listening on Facetime in their own homes, so none of the children will miss any of Nani's stories.

Layla, Musa Aaron, Seth has been waiting with great excitement.

"What story do you think Nani will tell us today boys", Layla asked her Brothers.

"Hmmmm, when she arrives, she will let us know", Musa responded.

"Have we got some banana cake left for Nani?", Aaron shouted to his mummy.

When Mummy replied she has, all the children helped her to cut slices of the banana cake they made the day before.

They all sat on their floor cushions with a slice of cake next to them waiting the arrival of their Nani.

Nani Serena arrived!

"Asalam alakium", Nani greeted everyone.

Walaikum asalam everyone responded.

The children cut a generous slice of the banana cake for Nani to have after the story-telling. Nani took up her seat on the floor cushion next to her cake.

"We were watching you on Facetime telling the story of Prophet Noah yesterday Nani", Layla told Nani Serena.

Nani started the session by asking the children what they learnt from the story of Prophet Noah.

Musa was the first to respond.

"Well if you break Allah's rules, then you will be punished. The bad people did not listen to Prophet Noah and forgot what Prophet Adam told them. They did not worship Allah but statutes."

It was now Aaron turn to give his understanding.

"But Allah is so merciful and send Prophet Noah to remind them. Allah gave them lots of chances, but they still did not listen. That's why Allah sent the floods and they all died.

"Well done children", Nani Serena praised the children.

Today Nani decided to tell the story of Prophet Hud and the people of the Land of Aad.

At that time the population on the earth grew larger and larger. The people who lived in Aad were descendants of Prophet Noah's grandson Iram.

They lived in a place between Oman and Yemen.

The people of Aad were tall and strong people. They worked very hard and build very large houses. They also build houses on top of the mountains. They were very wealthy and lived a good life.

They were pious and prayed to Allah.

Layla then asked some questions:

"Where was Shaitaan? Isn't his job to mislead people? When people are good and follow Allah's rules, he cant take them with him to the hellfire".

"You are so right Layla", Nani said in agreement.

Eventually, they did start worshipping idols. Shaitaan was very happy, knowing they will be joining him in the hellfire.

Then Allah sent Prophet Hud to remind the people about Allah's commands.

He pointed out their mistakes, but it fell on deaf ears. They really believed they can live a bad life because they did not believe in the Day of Judgement.

Layla quickly put her hand up eager to ask a question:

"And what is the Day of Judgement"?.

Journeying with the Prophets

Nani was very happy to answer.

Nani explained that the Day of Judgement is the Day when everyone will be brought back to life. The Day of Judgement will happen when the earth was like in the beginning when there was only Allah.

Allah will then bring back to life his creations - Humans, Angels, Jinns and animals. Some believe that on that day the animals will turn to dust and then Allah will start judgement day.

This is the day Allah will decide who will join Shaitaan in the hellfire.

"Those who break Allah's rules will be in the hellfire", informed Musa. "And the people of Aad who did not believe in the Day of Judgement will be in the hellfire"

In agreement with Musa, Nani continued her story.

The people of Aad was very much like the people of today. Many people in the world today are breaking Allah's rules and there are also some who laugh and make fun of the Muslims.

Allah orders that women must cover themselves, including their head. They laugh at Muslims who dress like that.

Muslims must pray 5 times a day and be very good and kind to everyone and share what you have. Many people break those rules too.

Allah tells us what to eat and not to eat pork. He also tells us about all the other food that we must not eat. Some decide themselves what is lawful and what's not. They assert that the day of Judgement is a belief only for fools and one must live life to the full, because when a person die, it's the end. They gave no regards to the hereafter.

Layla, the oldest of Nani Serena's grandchildren made a very astounding statement.

"That's why Allah sends the Coronavirus to remind us".

Nani was very proud of Layla to arrive at that understanding.

The people of Aad were very proud and arrogant.

When Prophet Hud reminded them that they will be asked on the Day of Judgement what they did, they laugh and made even more fun of him.

"That's because they did not believe in the Day of Judgement" said Seth.

Prophet Hud informed the people of Aad if their way of life continued

Allah will destroy them.

They were still doubtful.

Humankind then and present day do not understand why they are making this journey on earth, where they come from and where they will go. Allah sends his prophets to answers all these questions, even so some wanders blindly without accepting the guidance.

As the years passed the people of Aad became more and more proud and arrogant and even accused Prophet Hud of having mental problems. They believe their man-made Gods are responsible for his insanity.

Then Allah's punishment started coming.

First there was drought. The rain had stopped falling and the sun became hotter and hotter.

Even when Prophet Hud warned that it was the onset of the punishment to come they continued to laugh at him.

Then one day the clouds became dark and heavy. The people of Aad mistook it for rainfall, ending the drought period.

BUT THEY WERE WRONG

Instead of rain they were faced with very strong winds. Daily it became stronger and stronger. It whipped away people's clothing and ripped the skin off their bodies. It lasted for 8 days and 7 nights.

This environmental condition caused all the disbelievers and their massive dwellings to be reduced to dust, swallowed up by the sand in the desert.

Only the believers escaped this punishment, relocating to Yemen.

They live there in peace worshipping the one God.

Our next story will be PROPHET SALEH AND THE PEOPLE OF THAMUD. NANI SERENA WILL BE VISITING THE MAHMOODS FAMILY TO TELL THIS STORY.

SOURCES OF INFORMATION

Sources of Information

To the 'Ad People (We sent) Hud, one of their own brethren. He said: "O my people! worship Allah. ye have no other god but Him. (Your other gods) ye do nothing but invent! (Hud verse 50)

"O my people! I ask of you no reward for this (Message). My reward is from none but Him who created me: Will ye not then understand? (Hud verse 51)

"And O my people! Ask forgiveness of your Lord, and turn to Him (in repentance): He will send you the skies pouring abundant rain, and add strength to your strength: so turn ye not back in sin!" (Hud verse 52)

They said: "O Hud! No Clear (Sign) that hast thou brought us, and we are not the ones to desert our gods on thy word! Nor shall we believe in thee! (Hud verse 53)

"We say nothing but that (perhaps) some of our gods may have seized thee with imbecility." He said: "I call Allah to witness, and do ye bear witness, that I am free from the sin of ascribing, to Him, (Hud verse 54)

"Other gods as partners! so scheme (your worst) against me, all of you, and give me no respite. (Hud verse 55)

"I put my trust in Allah, My Lord and your Lord! There is not a moving creature, but He hath grasp of its fore-lock. Verily, it is my Lord that is on a straight Path. (Hud verse 56)

"If ye turn away,- I (at least) have conveyed the Message with which I was sent to you. My Lord will make another people to succeed you, and you will not harm Him in the least. For my Lord hath care and watch over all things." (Hud verse 57)

So when Our decree issued, We saved Hud and those who believed with him, by (special) Grace from Ourselves: We saved them from a severe penalty. (Hud verse 58)

And the chiefs of his people, who disbelieved and denied the Meeting in the Hereafter, and on whom We had bestowed the good things of this life, said: "He is no more than a man like yourselves: he eats of that of which ye eat, and drinks of what ye drink.

"If ye obey a man like yourselves, behold, it is certain ye will be lost (Al-Mu'minun verse 34)

"Does he promise that when ye die and become dust and bones, ye shall be brought forth (again)? (Al-Mu'minun verse 35)

"Far, very far is that which ye are promised! (Al-Mu'minun verse 36)

"There is nothing but our life in this world! We shall die and we live! But we shall never be raised up again! (Al-Mu'minun verse 37)

"He is only a man who invents a lie against Allah, but we are not the ones to believe in him!" (Al-Mu'minun verse 38)

(The prophet) said: "O my Lord! help me: for that they accuse me of falsehood." (Al-Mu'minun verse 39)

(Allah) said: "In but a little while, they are sure to be sorry!" (Al-Mu'minun verse 40)

Then the Blast overtook them with justice, and We made them as rubbish of dead leaves (floating on the stream of Time)! So away with the people who do wrong! (Al-Mu'minun verse 41)

And the 'Ad, they were destroyed by a furious Wind, exceedingly violent; (Al-Haqqah verse 6)

He made it rage against them seven nights and eight days in succession: so that thou couldst see the (whole) people lying prostrate in its (path), as they had been roots of hollow palm-trees tumbled down! (Al-Haqqah verse 7)

Then seest thou any of them left surviving? (Al-Haqqah verse 8)

Tasfeer of Ibn Kathir

CHAPTER 4

The People of Thamud-Prophet - Saleh (AS)

Nani Serena is now at the Mahmoods' with Keyaan, Leyah, Eva and Siyana.

Keyaan's opening sentence:

"Nani, we have been listening to you on Facetime telling the story of Prophet Noah and Prophet Hud. I can't wait today to hear the story of Prophet Saleh".

"That's right Keyaan, Nani Serena replied.

"Today I am going to tell you the story of Prophet Saleh. Before I start who can remind me about what we have learnt so far".

Leyah's hands went straight up.

Leyah with the most serious expression stared at everyone and started her recollections:

"I learnt that there is only one God and that's Allah. Allah is kind and merciful and created this world for us. He created the stars, the moon, the sun, the earth. He created everything on earth for us. Allah gives us rules to follow and we cannot break them. Shaitaan wants us to break them because when we do he will take us to the hellfire. On the day of judgement Allah will decide who will join Shaitaan in the hellfire".

"Masallah!! Masallah!!!", well done Leyah, Nani praised Leyah.

Before Nani Serena starts her story she asked the children to look on both shoulders and then asked what they saw.

"Nothing Nani. There is nothing on my shoulder Nani", said Siyana.

Nani went on to tell them that there are two angels sitting on each of the shoulders.

Journeying with the Prophets ■ 29

"Who can remember what I had said about the angels"? Nani asked.

It was now Eva's turn to answer:

"Angels are one of Allah's creations. They are like the Jinns. They can see us but we cannot see them". The Angels can only do what Allah tells them, but Jinns are like us as we can choose whether we do good or bad."

Nani praised Eva for her beautiful summary and proceeded to tell the children about the Angels on their shoulders.

Allah named these Angels Rakeeb and Ateeb. They have a very important job to do. They write down our good and bad deeds. Then on the Day of Judgement Allah will show us what they wrote about us.

Its very important if you do a bad deed you must ask Allah for forgiveness, and if you don't repeat that deed then the angels will remove it.

If you do a good deed then Allah will multiply it by 10, so you will have 10 good deeds instead of one.

"Allah loves us and is so merciful. He does not want Shaitaan to take us to hell with him, but we must not be disobedient", Keyaan informed everyone.

The story of the people of Thamud.

The people of Thamud was very similar to the people of Aad. Allah also bless them with good skills. Like the people of Aad they were very big and made beautiful houses. Some of these houses were on the mountain tops.

But as time goes by these people also stopped believing in Allah and started worshiping idols, stones, rocks.

Allah sent Prophet Saleh to remind them that what they are doing is very wrong. They did not listen to him.

One day Prophet Salih saw the people and their children worshipping a large stone. Prophet Saleh was very sad and continued to warn them about idol worshipping.

They laughed and jeered at him and told him to ask Allah to perform a miracle. They wanted a pregnant camel to emerge from the mountain.

Prophet Saleh asked them if Allah grants their wishes would they stop worshiping the idols and stones.

They said they will.

Allah granted their request.

They heard a very loud sound. The rocks were breaking apart and then there she was.

The pregnant camel was emerged.

It was huge.

The people were amazed. Some people believed the message of Prophet Saleh instantly. These were the poor people. But the rich people still did not believe and said it was just magic.

After a few days the camel gave birth to a beautiful baby camel. He followed his mother everywhere.

"I also followed my mummy everywhere", said little Siyana.

Days passed and the Camel and her baby ate the plants from the valley and drink water from the well. The camel produced lots of milk which she feeds to her baby.

The disbelievers of Thamud said they wanted the camel's milk as well.

Prophet Saleh and the people came to an agreement. They agreed that one day the camel will give her milk to them and on that day the camel and her baby can drink from the well.

Then on the following day she keeps her milk for her baby. This day the people and the other livestock can drink from the well.

First everyone was happy.

Then they began to complain that the camel drank too much water, or that she frightened their other livestock. Prophet Saleh began to fear that they might hurt the camel. He warned his people not to hurt the camel or else they will be punished.

With a sad face Keyaan said:

"Did they harm the camel Nani".

They did harm the camel.

As Nani Serena described how they killed the camel by piecing her with a sword and shooting her with an arrow, all the children had tears in their eyes.

"Will Allah punished the people Nani"? Keyaan sobbed.

"Well that was such an unkind thing to do" Leyah said sternly.

The two younger ones Eva and Siyana were crying for the baby camel because she hasn't got her mummy anymore.

Prophet Saleh was so sad and warned the people that Allah will send down his punishment in three days. He asked everyone to beg Allah for forgiveness. But they did not listen and even threatened to kill the prophet and his family.

"Did Allah punish them Nani?" Leyah asked.

"Yes, Leyah, Allah did. But he told Prophet Saleh and the believes to move out of Thamud and settled somewhere else".

Then after three days Allah sent his punishment.

There was thunder and lightning.

The earth shook violently. Allah destroyed the city of Thamud, and all the disbelievers died.

After they were destroyed, Prophet Salih addressed them. He said, "I endeavored to call you to the Religion of Islam. I invited you to the belief and to stop worshipping the idols. I tried to take you out of the dungeons of blasphemy to the light of Islam. I was keen in doing that. However, you turned me down and rejected my advice. You rejected what I called you to, and this is the result. The strong houses in the mountains, money, water, fertile land, and crops did not do you any good. Allah punished you for your blasphemy."

This story of Prophet Salih sheds light that Allah put us on this Earth and enabled us to benefit from the facilities and made us accountable. He sent Prophets and Messengers to tell us the rules. If people do not respond to the Prophet of their time, they are at a loss.

After the blasphemous people of Salih were destroyed, it is cited that Prophet Salih moved to the area of Ash-Sham, and lived in Palestine. Then he moved to Makkah and resided there worshipping God until he died.

Nani Serena's next Story will be Prophet Shoaib. She will be visiting her Yorkshire lads to tell this story.

SOURCES OF INFORMATION

And to the Thamud [We sent] their brother salih. He said, "O my people, worship Allah; you have no deity other than Him. There has come to you clear evidence from your Lord. This is the she-camel of Allah [sent] to you as a sign. So leave her to eat within Allah's land and do not touch her with harm, lest there seize you a painful punishment. (Al Araf verse 75)

Said the eminent ones who were arrogant among his people to those who were oppressed – to those who believed among them, "Do you [actually] know that salih is sent from his Lord?" They said, "Indeed we, in that with which he was sent, are believers.) (Al Araf verse 77)

So they hamstrung the she-camel and were insolent toward the command of their Lord and said, "O salih, bring us what you promise us, if you should be of the messengers (Hud verse 61)

And to Thamud [We sent] their brother salih. He said, "O my people, worship Allah; you have no deity other than Him. He has produced you from the earth and settled you in it, so ask forgiveness of Him and then repent to Him. Indeed, my Lord is near and responsive. (Hud verse 62)

They said, "O salih, you were among us a man of promise before this. Do you forbid us to worship what our fathers worshipped? And indeed we are, about that to which you invite us, in disquieting doubt (Hud verse 66)

So when Our command came, We saved salih and those who believed with him, by mercy from Us, and [saved them] from the disgrace of that day. Indeed, it is your Lord who is the Powerful, the Exalted in Might. (Hud verse 89)

And O my people, let not [your] dissension from me cause you to be struck by that similar to what struck the people of Noah or the people of Hud or the people of salih. And the people of Lot are not from you far away. (Al Shu'ara verse 142)

When their brother salih said to them, "Will you not fear Allah ? (Al Naml verse 45)

CHAPTER 5

The Story of Prophet Shoaib (AS)

Today Nani Serena is visiting her grandchildren in Halifax. It is indeed a very exciting time for her because she doesn't see the "Yorkshire" lads often. They live a very long way from Nani.

Omari and Zayn are very busy in the kitchen helping their mummy Sameena to prepare breakfast for their Nani.

When Nani arrived, she was presented with a mouth-watering breakfast. The aroma of this delicacy filled the air.

The masala beans, omelette with fried bread was very nicely presented on her plate. There was also a pot of desi tea. Nani love Desi tea.

Everyone enjoyed their breakfast.

Nani Serena began to tell the story.

"Who knows which story I will be telling today?", Nani asked the boys.

With a cheeky smile on Omari face he answered:

"You will be telling the Story of Prophet Shoaib. Do you know Nani that our family name is Shoaib?"

"Yes Omari, I do know that."

Zayn seemed to be getting rather impatient. So, Nani started her story.

A very long time ago in a place called Midan, there lived a very old man. His name was Prophet Shoaib. Today Midan is called Syria.

Prophet Shoaib was a very good man and he worshipped only Allah.

Others in Midan did not.

They were bandits and thieves. Even though they had a good life they stole from each other. They would even steal from the

visitors that pass through their town. Nothing was enough for them. The more they have, the more they want. They were ungrateful people.

The shop keepers were no better. They were very deceptive. They sold defective goods, short changed people.

Accumulation of wealth took precedence in their lives.

And instead of worshipping one God, they worshipped trees.

"Nani, there are people like those living in Halifax now. They also tell lies and cheat their customers", informed Zayn.

"And some bad people even went to prison because they cheated some old people", added Omari.

Nani thanked the children for their input.

So Allah sent Prophet Shoaib.

The prophet tried to guide the people and explained that they must only worship God, and the importance of honesty.

He told them to stop their thieving and robbing.

"Did they listen to him"? asked Omari.

"No! Only a few did. They said it's the practice of their forefathers and will not stop. They even told the prophet if they did, their wealth will decrease", explained Nani Serena.

The prophet reminded them that he only wanted the best for them but still they took no heed.

As the prophet continued calling them to follow Allah's rules, they began threatening to hurt him.

And then one day they threw the prophet and his followers out of the city.

They jeered and taunted him to bring the punishment of Allah.

THEN IT ALL CHANGED

The punishment came. Allah made the sun very hot in Midan. There was severe drought. It was like that for seven days.

The people were now suffering and no matter what they did to cool themselves they were still burning.

By now all the water in the wells dried up. And all the plants died.

The wicked people of Midan were being punished.

When a huge black cloud appeared in the sky, they began to rejoice. They were relieved, thinking there will be a heavy rainfall

BUT THEY WERE WRONG. IT WAS THE PUNISHMENT FROM ALLAH

There was a huge thunderstorm. As it swept through the city of Midan the earth started shaking violently. The people started falling.

Huge balls of fire descended from the sky.

Everyone was burnt to ashes.

Like the people of Aad, their entire civilization was destroyed.

Now, it was time for Nani Serena to leave her Yorkshire lads, but promised to return to tell another story.

SOURCE OF INFORMATION

The leaders, the arrogant party among his people, said: "O Shu'aib! we shall certainly drive thee out of our city - (thee) and those who believe with thee; or else ye (thou and they) shall have to return to our ways and religion." He said: "What! even though we do detest (them)? (Al Araf verse 88)

89. "We should indeed invent a lie against Allah, if we returned to your ways after Allah hath rescued us therefrom; nor could we by any manner of means return thereto unless it be as in the will and plan of Allah, Our Lord. Our Lord can reach out to the utmost recesses of things by His knowledge. In the Allah is our trust. our Lord! decide Thou between us and our people in truth, for Thou art the best to decide." (Al Araf verse 89)

90. The leaders, the unbelievers among his people, said: "If ye follow Shu'aib, be sure then ye are ruined!" (Al Araf verse 90)

91. But the earthquake took them unawares, and they lay prostrate in their homes before the morning! (Al Araf verse 91)

92. The men who reject Shu'aib became as if they had never been in the homes where they had flourished: the men who rejected Shu'aib - it was they who were ruined! (Al Araf verse 92)

93. So Shu'aib left them, saying: "O my people! I did indeed convey to you the messages for which I was sent by my Lord: I gave you good counsel, but how shall I lament over a people who refuse to believe!" (Al Araf verse 93) 84.

To the Madyan People (We sent) Shu'aib, one of their own brethren: he said: "O my people! worship Allah. Ye have no other god but Him. And give not short measure or weight: I see you in prosperity, but I fear for you the penalty of a day that will compass (you) all round. 84. To the Madyan People (We sent) Shu'aib, one of their own brethren: he said: "O my people! worship Allah. Ye have no other god but Him. And give not short measure or weight: I see you in prosperity, but I fear for you the penalty of a day that will compass (you) all round. 84. To the Madyan People (We sent) Shu'aib, one of their own brethren: he said: "O my people! worship Allah. Ye have no other god but Him. And give not short measure or weight: I see you in prosperity, but I fear for you the penalty of a day that will compass (you) all round.(Al Hud verse 84)

And O my people! give just measure and weight, nor withhold from the people the things that are their due: commit not evil in the land with intent to do mischief. .(Al Hud verse 85)

That which is left you by Allah is best for you, if ye (but) believed! but I am not set over you to keep watch!" .(Al Hud verse 86)

They said: "O Shu'aib! Does thy (religion of) prayer command thee that we leave off the worship which our fathers practised, or that we leave off doing what we like with our property? truly, thou art the one that forbeareth with faults and is right-minded!" .(Al Hud verse 87)

He said: "O my people! see ye whether I have a Clear (Sign) from my Lord, and He hath given me sustenance (pure and) good as from Himself? I wish not, in opposition to you, to do that which I forbid you to do. I only desire (your) betterment to the best of my power; and my success (in my task) can only come from Allah. In Him I trust, and unto Him I look. .(Al Hud verse 88)

And O my people! let not my dissent (from you) cause you to sin, lest ye suffer a fate similar to that of the people of Noah or of Hud or of Salih, nor are the people of Lut far off from you! .(Al Hud verse 89)

But ask forgiveness of your Lord, and turn unto Him (in repentance): For my Lord is indeed full of mercy and loving-kindness." .(Al Hud verse 90)

They said: "O Shu'aib! much of what thou sayest we do not understand! In fact among us we see that thou hast no strength! Were it not for thy family, we should certainly have stoned thee! for thou hast among us no great position!" .(Al Hud verse 91)

He said: "O my people! is then my family of more consideration with you than Allah. For ye cast Him away behind your backs (with contempt). But verily my Lord encompasseth on all sides all that ye do! .(Al Hud verse 92)

And O my people! Do whatever ye can: I will do (my part): Soon will ye know who it is on whom descends the penalty of ignominy; and who is a liar! and watch ye! for I too am watching with you!" .(Al Hud verse 93)

When Our decree issued, We saved Shu'aib and those who believed with him, by (special) mercy from Ourselves: But the (mighty) blast did seize the wrong- doers, and they lay prostrate in their homes by the morning, .(Al Hud verse 94)

As if they had never dwelt and flourished there! Ah! Behold! How the Madyan were removed (from sight) as were removed the Thamud!. (Al Hud verse 95)

Tasfeer of Ibn Kathir

CHAPTER 6

The Story of Prophet Ibraheem (AS), (Abraham), and Ishmael (AS)

Today Nani Serena is visiting Jasmine, Tariq and Amelia to tell the story of Prophet Ibraheem.

Nani Serena started telling the story.

A long, long time ago in Iraq in the city of Babylon lived a man called Azar. He was from the descendants of Shem, son of Noah. He was a very good sculpture and carved idols from stones. People buy these idols and pray to them. There were so many of them in the temples, all nicely decorated. The people would even give them food.

"But idols cannot eat", said Jasmine.

"They cannot do anything, except remain where the people will leave them", piped up Tariq.

"They are like my dolls", added Amelia. "I only pretend to feed them because I know they cannot not eat. How come the people did not know that the idols cannot do anything? Did everyone believe that the idols were God"? continued Amelia.

Nani told the children that Azar had a son name Ibraheem and he did not believe that the idols were Gods.

One day when he saw his father carving a large idol, he began to ask him some questions. He wanted to know why these idols that he plays were in the temple and the people were praying to them.

The father was unable to give any sensible explanations.

Azar named this big statute Marduk. Marduk had very large ears. He explained to Ibraheem that the large ears meant that he is very knowledgeable.

With a stunned look on Jasmine's face she informed:

"Well, I am puzzled as Ibraheem is.

So, if Azar had put small ears on him then it would have very little knowledge?" asked Tariq.

"Hmmm, its like Azar is the one who can decide how much knowledge these Idols have", added Amelia.

When Ibraheem was sixteen years old he went to look for Allah.

He walked a very long way until he saw a mountain. He climbed up and sat right at the top.

He remained there until it was dark. When Ibraheem saw a very large star he thought it might be Allah but when the star disappeared, and replaced by the moon he wondered if the moon was Allah. But when daylight came and the sun appeared he thought the Sun might be Allah as it was bigger. When the sun also disappeared at nightfall he knew that it wasnt.

Ibraheem realised that the one who creates everything must be the one true God, and the stars, the moon and the sun were all Allah's creations.

He then knelt and pray to the one God, Allah. He knew then that he was a prophet and Allah had chosen him to guide the people.

So Prophet Ibraheem went on to educate the people.

"Did they all stop worshiping the idols after Prophet Ibraheem told them about Allah"? Jasmine enquired.

Nani Serena responded that Prophet Ibraheem's father became very angry with him and did not believe him. He shouted at the prophet and told him to leave his house.

When he went to the others and told them about Allah, they also did not believe him and told him to go away.

There came a day when there was a big festival. Prophet Ibraheem thought of a plan. He wanted to show the uselessness of the idols.

He seized his opportunity and use an axe to destroy all the idols except the large one. He then hung the axe over its head.

"That was indeed a very brave thing to do" said Tariq.

"The people must have been very angry when they returned, Amelia added".

Serena Husain Yates

Nani Serena went on to explain what happened afterwards.

When the people returned from the festival, they were furious. They knew that it was Prophet Ibraheem who broke all the idols.

To prove a point, he told them that the large remaining idol was responsible.

His point was proven, when the disbelievers in anger shouted that a statue is not capable of doing anything.

The point was put across, yet they people did not believe.

The prophet was to receive a punishment. Death. They were going to burn him alive. They made a huge fire. The heat was so fierce that it can only be viewed from a distance.

Then the day arrived that Prophet was going to be thrown into that pit of fire.

(There was some extra letters here which I deleted) The day of this injustice came. The burning of the young Prophet.

The crowd gathered in droves, laughing, jeering, clapping. It was as if this was the biggest excitement of their lives.

Just before this occurrence, Prophet Ibraheem had a visitor. It was an angel. He was sent by Allah to ask him to make a wish. Instead of requesting that the people would change their mind, he only wished that Allah should be pleased with him.

When they put him in the fire he yelled:

"Allah is sufficient for me."

All three children were looking very distressed by now. But Nani Serena told them about the miracle that had taken place.

THE FIRE DID NOT BURN PROPHET IBRAHEEM. HE WALKED OUT UNHARMED.

The realisation came to a few. Is the prophet to be believed about the existence of one God!!They had just witnessed a miracle. It can only be the God of Ibraheem that saved him.

Unfortunately, others were still in a state of ignorance and decide the only course of action would be to take him to the King of the land, King Nimrod.

Infront of the King Prophet Ibraheem explained himself very well. He told about the worshipping of false gods. He proclaimed the existence of one God who is almighty and its only him who can decide whether a person live or die.

Instead of the king believing him the conceited king showed his arrogance when he said he can give life and death.

All the children gasped on hearing this.

He called for two of his subjects. He killed one and spared the life of the other.

He was very pleased with himself and the power he can exercised.

Prophet Ibraheem challenged him to make the sun raise from the west as Allah makes it raise from the east.

As King Nimrod could not make that happen, he let the prophet go.

Prophet Ibraheem continued his mission. The obstinate people refused to believe. He only had two followers, Lut, who was his nephew and Sarah. She later became his wife.

PROPHET IBRAHEEM, LUT AND SARAH LEFT BABYLON

After the disbelief of the people continued, the prophet left Babylon. He travelled to Syria, Palestine and Egypt to continue his preaching.

In this journey they did many good deeds by helping the needy.

Lut left the duo to live in a place by the dead sea.

Prophet Ibraheem and Sarah continued their journey until they reached a land where an evil king lived.

This evil king heard about the new traveller and his beautiful wife, Sarah. He asked his guards to bring them to him.

Prophet Ibraheem went first and when questioned who Sarah was, he replied she was his sister. He said this to protect her.

It was now Sarah's turn to meet the king.

The evil king was amazed at her beauty and tried to touch her. By the will of Allah his hand froze. He asked Sarah to pray to Allah to make him better and promised not to harm her. Sarah prayed, he recovered. He tried to touch her again, and once again his hand was immobile. This time he promised Sarah if Allah was to make him better he will not repeat the behaviour.

He kept his promise. He realised that Sarah must be very special. He released the couple and gifted them a slave girl called Hajrah.

The years went by and they all got very old. Prophet Ibraheem and Sarah longed for children but were not blessed with any.

Sarah then gave her husband permission to marry Hajrah, who went on to have a child with the prophet.

A CHILD WAS BORN

Hajrah gave birth to a son and they called him Ishmael. When Ishmael was just a baby Allah told Ibraheem to take Hajrah and the baby on a long journey.

They travelled for many days and nights until they came to Mountain Marwa.

Prophet Ibraheem left them all alone in the desert. Apart from some water and dates, they had no food . Everywhere was barren.

She called out to the prophet to ask his intentions. When he didn't reply she knew that her circumstance was by the will of Allah. She has firm belief in Allah and was not afraid.

Prophet Ibraheem was very sad to leave his family and place his entire trust in Allah. Though in grief, he knew his family will be looked after.

Eventually the food and water ran out.

Hajrah began to run between the two mountains Safa and Marwah, shouting for help. No help came as there was no one.

She continued running between the mountains seven times.

She then heard a voice!!!

Allah had sent an Angel. The angel took his wings and dug the earth until there was flowing water.

She was overjoyed. Her thirst was well and truly quenched.

"Alhumdulliah, Subhanallah", said Jasmine.

"Allah can do anything. We must not be afraid because when you believe in Allah, he will help you in all situations", Tariq addressed the children.

"I will always believe in Allah", Amelia replied.

That water is the ZamZam water. It is a very special water and that well is still there in present day time.

They were later joined by some travellers who were also looking for water.

These were the first settlers there.

The few settlers gave raise to a community of people.

Ishmael grew up to be a very pious person and married one of the local girls.

The time had come when Prophet Ibraheem went looking for his family.

He arrived to find a very different community. There was no longer barren land with no inhabitants, but a thriving community with fertile land.

He found out that his wife Hajrah had died but Ismael was still alive.

Son and father was so happy to finally reconnect.

Serena Husain Yates

PROPHET IBRAHEEM HAD TO FACE ANOTHER TEST FROM ALLAH

The prophet saw in a dream that he must sacrifice his son. Initially, he was dismissive, but it became a recurring dream. He knew that this will be his toughest trial.

In deep thought Tariq told:

"Prophet Ibraheem had many trials and tests. First he was thrown in the fire, then he had to leave his family in the desert and now he has to kill his son."

Jasmine reassuringly said:

"But Allah helped and protected him in all the trials."

When Prophet Ibraheem told his son about his dream, Ishmael reassured his father that he must obey Allah.

They journeyed to Mount Arafat to perform this sacrifice.

Ishmael requested that his father tie his legs and hands so he will not struggle.

The prophet obliged and wore a blindfold so that he will not witness the suffering of his child.

The prophet had passed his test. Allah sent a lamb instead for the sacrifice.

The prophet was also rewarded with a second son. His wife Sarah gave birth and the child was called Ishaaq.

Nani will tell the story of Ishaaq next.

SOURCE OF INFORMATION

(Al-An'am) Verses 75-80

(Al-Anbiya) Verses 62-63

(Al-Anbiya) Verses 65-66

(Al-Baqarah) Verse 260

Tasfeer of Ibn Kathir

CHAPTER 7

The Story of Prophet Ishaaq (AS) and Prophet Yaqub (AS)

As promised, Nani Serena has returned to the Yates grandchildren to tell the story of Prophet Ishaaq and Prophet Yaqub.

"Who can tell me what they learnt from the story of Prophet Ibrahim"? asked Nani Serena.

All hands went up. The children were so eager to tell.

Jasmine started her recount:

"Prophet Ibraheem went through many trials and passed all of them. I felt sad when he had to leave his wife and baby in the desert all alone. But I felt happy when Allah sent the ZamZam water and many people to live there with them.

Tariq's recount:

"I felt sad when Prophet Ibraheem was asked to sacrifice his son Ishmael. My second name is also Ishmael. Then I was so happy when Allah sent the sheep from heaven".

Now it was Amelia's turn:

"I felt sad when the bad people built a fire to burn Prophet Ibraheem, but happy when the fire turn cool".

So as promised Nani Serena began to tell the story of Prophet Ishaaq.

One day when Prophet Ibraheem and his wife were very old, they had three visitors. These were angels sent to them from Allah.

They came to tell them that they were going to have a son and his name will be Ishaaq and he will be a prophet.

They were so happy. Sarah told the angels that she was very surprised because she was old and did not think that she would be able to have children. The angels reassured her that everything is possible with the blessings of Allah.

Prophet Ishaaq was born and grew up to be a very pious child following all of Allah's commandments.

As Prophet Ibraheem was getting older and older he wanted his son to get marry before he died.

They were living in a place called Canaan. Today its known to be part of Israel and Syria. The people in Canaan were disbelievers so he sent one of his servants to a place called Haran to choose a bride for Prophet Ishaaq. Some people believe that Harran is now called Turkey. But Allah knows best.

The servant chose a girl named Rebekkah to be the bride for Prophet Ishaaq. Rebekkah was the daughter of Ibn Nahoor. He was the brother of Prophet Ibraheem.

They got married and prayed to Allah for a child. After a very long time Allah blessed them with a set of twins. They were called Esau and Prophet Yaqub.

They were always fighting with each other because Esau believed that his father loved Prophet Yaqub more than him.

Many years had passed and when Ishaaq was very sick he made a request to his son Esau. He asked for him to cook a meal for him, choosing meat from one of his finest sheep.

Unfortunately, Rebekkah asked Prophet Yaqub to do the same. Prophet Yaqub presented his father with the meal. Prophet Ishaaq enjoyed his spread and chose Yaqub to be the leader of the people.

Of course, when Esau returned, Prophet Ishaaq had already eaten from Prophet Yaqub and had chosen his leader. Esau was very angry about the situation and threatened to hurt brother.

Rebekkah quickly sent Prophet Yaqub to live with her brother Laban in a place called Charan.

The journey to Charan was a very long one. After awhile Yaqub felt very tired, put a stone under his head and fell asleep.

He dreamt of a stairs leading up to heaven where he saw a group of angels who were coming down to earth and then climbing back to heaven.

It was a very nice dream and Yaqub made a promise to himself to build a mosque there when he returned to his homeland. He poured some oil on the stone so he would be able to recognise it on his return. This place is now called Jerusalem.

It was then that Allah blessed Yaqub with this land and all of his future generations.

THE DAUGHTERS OF LABAN

Laban had two daughters. The older one was Leyah and the younger one was Rachel.

Yaqub wanted to marry Rachel. Her father Laban told him if he worked in his land for seven years he would agree to the marriage.

Yaqub worked hard for seven years and was very happy at the end. He was looking forward to getting married to Rachel.

"Did he marry Rachel"? asked Jasmine.

"No, Jasmine. Laban tricked him into marrying his older daughter Leyah instead and told Yaqub that he had to work another seven years before he could marry Rachel", explained Nani Serena.

"That's not a very nice thing to do", said Tariq sympathetically.

"What did he do Nani? Did he work for another seven years"? asked Amelia.

"Yes, he did Amelia", Nani replied.

So now we have Prophet Yaqub nicely married and settled with two wives.

As time goes by Prophet Yaqub's wife Leyah had many sons but Rachel had none. She prayed to Allah and she was blessed with two sons. Prophet Yusuf and Beniyamin.

PROPHET YAQUB AND HIS FAMILY RETURNED TO HIS HOMELAND, HEBRON.

It was now time for the prophet to return to his homeland. He told his uncle Laban of his intentions. Laban was happy. He told the prophet that since he had worked very hard for him to ask for whatever he wanted. Prophet Yaqub asked for all the black and black speckled sheep.

Tariq then asked Nani Serena:

"Did his uncle give him what he wanted?"

Laban did not keep his promise. In fact, he tricked the prophet again. One day when the prophet wasn't there Laban and his sons removed all the black and speckled sheep and only left the white ones.

Prophet Yaqub was very disappointed because his uncle had tricked him once again.

He made duas to Allah. And in the next season all the lambs that were born were either black or black and speckled.

Laban became very worried now because he knew that all the new flock now belonged to Prophet Yaqub.

The day arrived that they must leave. Prophet Yaqub left with his wives and family and took everything that belonged to him, including the livestock. He did not tell his uncle of his plans.

When Laban realised that the prophet had left, he took all his servants and went looking for them. After several days they spotted them.

When they finally caught up Laban spoke of his disappointment of not saying farewell to his daughters and grandchildren.

There and then they had a feast and before they bid their farewell Prophet Yaqub requested that after this meeting to never meet up again. They must not enter each other land.

Everyone agreed on this and parted ways.

It was a very long way back to his homeland and so they took their tents with them. One night when Prophet Yaqoob was sitting in front of his tent an angel visited him and told him to change his name to Israel.

And that's where the name of the country came from.

When the prophet reached his homeland, he sent a message to his brother Esau to ask for his forgiveness.

"Oh, I know who Esau is", said Amelia proudly. "He is the prophet's twin brother that he ran away from because he tricked him".

"Well done Amelia, that's right. You remembered", Nani said, looking at Amelia fondly.

Esau decided to take his men to meet up with his brother. When Prophet Yaqub learnt of this he was afraid. He thought his brother will hurt him and prayed to Allah. He was sorry that he had tricked his brother and wanted to give him some gifts.

He sent the gifts with his servants.

"What were the gifts"? Tariq asked.

"Two hundred goats, 200 lambs and 30 camels", replied Nani Serena.

Jasmine with a big smile on her face spoke:

"I guess Esau was very happy with so much gifts".

Nani replied that he was, although in the beginning he didn't want to accept as he felt that his brother was being too generous.

After several days of walking Prophet Yaqub and his brother Esau finally met.

Esau ran to the prophet, embrace him and started to cry. He was so happy.

Prophet Yaqub introduced his children to his brother and refer to them as gifts from Allah.

"Nani, you always say that about all of your grandchildren", said Jasmine.

Jasmin was right. All children are gifts to their parents from Allah.

As they were all making their way back Prophet Yaqub saw the rock that he poured the oil on.

"Yes, yes, I remembered Tariq shouted excitedly. Prophet Yaqub said on his return he will build a mosque. It was in Jerusalem."

Tariq was correct and the prophet built a mosque. That was the first mosque built in Jerusalem.

They continued their journey to Hebron which was the prophet homeland. Today many Palestinians live in Hebron. It is their largest city.

Prophet Ishaaq was still alive and was so happy to meet his son, daughter-in-laws and all his grandchildren.

It was the first time he had seen his family after such a long time. In those days there was no Facetime, mobile phones, or even land lines. People will walk or rode on camels if they wanted to deliver messages.

Prophet Ishaaq lived a few more years and then died. He was one hundred and eighty years old. He was buried next to his father Prophet Ibraheem.

Prophet Yaqub had twelve sons and they are referred to as Bani Israel. This means that they are the children of Israel.

One of his sons was Yusuf. He is a very important prophet in Islam and a whole chapter of the Quran is named after him.

Tomorrow children I will tell you the Story of Prophet Yusuf.

SOURCES OF INFORMATION

We gave him Ishaq and Ya'qub. Each of them We made a Prophet. And We gave them of Our mercy and assigned to them a high and true renown. (Maryam verse: 49-50)

And We gave him tidings of the birth of Ishaq, a Prophet of the righteous and We showered Our blessings on him and on Ishaq and of their offspring are some who do good and some who plainly wrong their own selves. (As Saaffat: 113)

The same did Abraham enjoin upon his sons, and also Ya'qub (saying): O' my sons! Lo! Allah has chosen for you the true religion, therefore die not save as men who have surrendered (unto Him) or were you present when death came to Ya'qub when he said to his sons:

What will you worship after me? They said: We shall worship your God, God of your fathers, Abraham and Ishaq, One God and unto Him we have surrendered." (Surah Baqarah 132-133)

Or were you witnesses when death approached Jacob, when he said to his sons, What will you worship after me?" They said, "We will worship your God and the God of your fathers, Abraham and Ishmael and Isaac – one God. And we are Muslims [in submission] to Him. (Surah Baqarah 136)

Say, [O believers], "We have believed in Allah and what has been revealed to us and what has been revealed to Abraham and Ishmael and Isaac and Jacob and the Descendants and what was given to Moses and Jesus and what was given to the prophets from their Lord. We make no distinction between any of them, and we are Muslims [in submission] to Him. (Surah Baqarah 140)

Or do you say that Abraham and Ishmael and Isaac and Jacob and the Descendants were Jews or Christians? Say, "Are you more knowing or is Allah ?" And who is more unjust than one who conceals a testimony he has from Allah ? And Allah is not unaware of what you do. (Al Imran verse 84)

And his Wife was standing, and she smiled. Then We gave her good tidings of Isaac and after Isaac, Jacob.(Yusuf verse 6)

And thus will your Lord choose you and teach you the interpretation of narratives and complete His favor upon you and upon the family of Jacob, as He completed it upon your fathers before, Abraham and Isaac. Indeed, your Lord is Knowing and Wise. (Yusuf verse 38)

Who will inherit me and inherit from the family of Jacob. And make him, my Lord, pleasing [to You].(Maryam verse 49)

So when he had left them and those they worshipped other than Allah , We gave him Isaac and Jacob, and each [of them] We made a prophet. (Al-Anbiyah)

And We gave to Him Isaac and Jacob and placed in his descendants prophethood and scripture. And We gave him his reward in this world, and indeed, he is in the Hereafter among the righteous. (Sad verse 45)

TASFEER OF IBN KATHIR

CHAPTER 8

The Story of Prophet Yusuf (Joseph)

Today Nani Serena will be telling the story of Prophet Yusuf to the Arshad Family. Layla, Musa, Aaron and Seth love listening to Nani's stories. They are so happy that their Nani today can tell the story in person rather than through Facetime. Of course, the other grandchildren will be joining virtually.

"Who can tell me what they have learnt from the Story of Prophet Yaqub"? asked Nani Serena.

All hands went up. Layla was the first to speak:

"Prophet Yaqub was the grandson of Prophet Ibraheem. His father's name was Prophet Ishaaq and he had a twin brother name Esau.

It was now Musa's turn:

"Prophet Yaqub went to live with his uncle Laban in Charan. This was because he tricked his brother Esau and was afraid that he will be hurt by him. On the journey he was tired and placed a rock under his head and fell asleep. He had a beautiful dream and promised to build a mosque there when he returned. That place is now called Jerusalem".

"It's now my turn", said Aaron. "Prophet Yaqub was married to both Leyah and Rachel".

"Now what will you like to say Seth", Nani fondly asked her youngest grandchild.

"They had twelve sons. His second wife had two sons, Benyameen and Prophet Yusuf.

Nani Serena was very happy that the children remembered the story.

Nani Serena started to tell her story.

Prophet Yusuf and his mummy Rachel were the most beautiful people on earth. Prophet Yaqub loved his young son very much because he had such good qualities and was also very protective of him.

One day Prophet Yusuf had a dream. He dreamt that the sun, the moon and eleven stars bowed before him. His father knew straightaway that this dream meant that he was a prophet. He told his son not to mention his dream to his brothers because they are very jealous and will hurt him.

But the young prophet told his brothers of the dream. They were very angry. They even thought about killing him.

But then they came up with another idea. They plan to take him to a well and leave him in it.

The children all gasped with sadness on their faces.

So, one day the evil brothers persuaded their father to let Prophet Yusuf accompany them to the fields where they farmed. At first the father didn't agree because he was afraid that the brothers will hurt him. But after reassuring him that they will take good care of the young prophet he gave his permission.

"And did they leave him the well?" asked Musa.

"Yes, they did Musa", replied Nani Serena.

"Prophet Yusuf must have been very scared in the well" said Layla.

"That's right Layla, replied Nani, "Prophet Yusuf was only a young boy and he was so scared in that deep well. He spent many nights and days there".

And then one day there were some travellers looking water and found the Prophet.

"Did they return him to his father? Asked Aaron.

But Nani told the children they did not.

These travellers were not good people. They put him in chains and took him to Egypt to sell him as a slave.

Journeying with the Prophets

Seth was so sad on hearing what they did to the prophet and with his eyes filling up with tears he asked:

"What happened to him"?

Nani told the children that the young prophet was taken to the market to be sold as a slave. The market was full of people and they were all amazed how beautiful Prophet Yusuf was. Everyone wanted to buy him.

The prophet was bought by the Aziz of Egypt. He gave them a small bag of silver coins and took the prophet to his palace.

He removed his chains and told the Prophet Yusuf he could live with his family, but he must never betray his trust.

The prophet lived happily in the palace for awhile.

But then it all changed.

The Aziz's wife, Zulaika, made up lies about the young prophet. She told that he tried to kiss her.

The fact of the matter was she tried to seduce him and as he was running away from her she grabbed his shirt from the back tearing it.

At the same time the door opened. It was her husband, the Aziz. and his friends.

Zulaika tried to lie to everyone that it was the prophet who had tried to seduce her. But they knew she was lying because his shirt was torn from the back.

Nonetheless, some of the news of this incident got to the women friends of Zulaika and the women started to talk about the incident. They mocked her saying that she lusted after one whom they thought was a young, lowly slave. They had not seen Yusuf yet.

A furious Zulaika got news of the gossiping, so she came up with a plan. She invited these women to her home. She prepared a meal and gave them each a knife. As the women started cutting their fruits, Zulaika invited Yusuf in the room. When the women saw Yusuf they were so entranced by his beauty that they began to cut their hands with the knives without noticing. They exclaimed, "This is not a human, but a generous angel!" At that, Zulaika told them, "This is the man about whom you blame me. I tried to seduce him, but he refused."

The evil woman then told Yusuf he if doesn't do what she asked him to do she will put him in prison. To that Prophet Yusuf replied:

"The prison is more dear to me than sinning." Joseph made duas to Allah to relieve him from the scheming of the women, and to make him pure from sin. Allah fulfilled Joseph's supplication.

Zulaika became enraged and lied to her husband. She told him that the prophet had told all the women of her seduction and demanded he be imprisoned.

Although the Aziz had liked Yusuf, he wanted the accusations against his wife to settle down and had the prophet imprisoned.

PROPHET YUSUF WAS IN PRISON

In prison everyone was amazed how beautiful the prophet was. They thought that he was an angel.

Whilst in prison Allah blessed him with the ability to interpret dreams.

Soon, there was two new inmates, the cook and the cupbearer. They wanted the prophet to interpret their dreams.

The cook dreamt that there was some bread on top of his head and two birds were eating it.

The prophet prayed to Allah and then told him that it means that he will be crucified until he died.

The cupbearer then told of his dream. He dreamt that he was in the palace serving the king.

Again, Prophet Yusuf prayed and interpreted his dream. He told the cupbearer that he will be a free man and will work in the palace again.

Both of his interpretations came through. Before the cupbearer was set free, Prophet Yusuf told him to tell the king that he was wrongfully put into prison and must be freed.

Unfortunately, Shaitan made the cupbearer forgot the message and he didn't tell the king of this injustice.

Prophet Yusuf remained in prison for a few more years.

One night the king had a very frightening dream. He saw that he was standing on the bank on the River Nile and all the water had gone. There was only mud. The fishes were gasping for breath because there was no water.

After that he saw that Nile had water again and seven fat cows were coming out from the water. Afterwards, seven lean cows came out.

All the lean cows were swallowed by the fat ones.

Then he saw seven years of green corns growing by the riverbank. It then disappeared with seven years of withered corns.

No one in the palace was able to interpret the king's dreams.

It was then cupbearer remembered Prophet Yusuf.

He told the king about the prophet. He related how the prophet interpreted his and the other prisoner's dreams. He also told of the great injustice that Prophet Yusuf had suffered.

The king commanded the cupbearer to meet with the prophet and to ask him to interpret his dream.

This he did. Prophet Yusuf then prayed to Allah. He gave the interpretation as follows:

- Seven years of rich harvest in the kingdom and people will have plenty of food.

- Then there will be seven years of drought in the kingdom and people will not have enough in Egypt and all the neighbouring lands.

The king was very pleased with the interpretation and demanded that Prophet Yusuf set free.

"Was he released then Nani", asked Layla.

"No", Nani answered. "The prophet wanted his innocence to be proven so he refused to leave the prison" Nani continued.

"What happened then"? enquired Musa.

Nani went on to tell the children what took place.

The King ordered an enquiry and summoned Zulaika and the gossiping women. This time she told the truth and finally Prophet Yusuf was set free from prison.

The king was very impressed by the prophet's knowledge and asked for more information about his dream.

Prophet Yusuf advised that the king should plan for the famine ahead.

He also told the king that the famine will not only affect Egypt but all the neighbouring countries.

The king was so impressed by Prophet Yusuf that he appointed him to work in the Kingdom. He was put in charge of the grainery. His job was to guard the harvest and make plans for the upcoming famine.

In the seven prosperous years all the crops were harvested and stored so when the period of famine will begin there will be enough food.

PROPHET YUSUF MET HIS BROTHERS

The famine period had started. There was severe drought and all the crops died. But the people were not hungry because the Prophet planned well. There were more than enough grains stored to feed not only the people of Egypt but the neighbouring lands as well.

"I guess the king was very happy with Prophet Yusuf because of the plentiful food", related Layla.

"He was Layla", voiced Nani. "But the humble prophet refused to take any credit. He said it was all from Allah".

The people in the nearby land made no plans for this famine and they had no food. The kind prophet advised the king to sell the grains to them very cheaply as everything they have is from Allah. In that way they will save many lives.

The king listened and did exactly what the prophet advised.

This drought spread to Canaan (Jerusalem) where the prophet's family lived.

News reached them about the abundance of grains being distributed in Egypt. Prophet Yaqub sent ten of his sons to go to Egypt to buy the grains.

"Didn't Benyamin go"? enquired Musa.

"Prophet Yaqub didn't want to send his youngest child with them, replied Nani. "He suffered a lot when Prophet Yusuf didn't return home all those years ago.

When the brothers arrived at the palace Prophet Yusuf recognised them straightaway, but they did not know him. He gave them the grains and asked after his younger brother Benyameen. The brothers told him that their father will not allow to take him with them.

The prophet suggested that they bring Benyameen and he will double the supply of grains.

The prophet then did a very kind thing. He returned their gold coins by hiding them in one of the grain sack.

They went home and related their experience to their father.

Despite hearing the brothers' story, Prophet Yaqub still refused to let Benyameen accompany the brothers. He never forgot what they did to Prophet Yusuf.

But it came to a point when they had no choice as all the grains had ran out. Prophet Yusuf had told the brothers they must never re-enter Egypt without Benyameen.

Prophet Yaqub finally agreed.

So all eleven brothers set out for Egypt.

When Prophet Yusuf saw his little brother, he was so happy. Tears welled up in his eyes.

A big feast was prepared in the palace for the brothers. Benyameen sat next to his older brother. He looked so sad and told Prophet Yusuf how much he missed his brother.

When Prophet Yusuf was alone with him, he embraced him and revealed his identity. They cried in each other arms.

They agreed for the time being their relationship will remain a secret.

The next day arrived and the brothers were preparing to make their journey home. Prophet Yusuf felt very sad because he will miss his little brother. So, he thought of a clever plan.

He placed the King's golden cup in Benyameen's grain sack. He hoped that his brother will be accused of stealing and hence he will remain in the palace with him.

His plan worked. The brothers were very sad. The eldest brother Judaa begged Prophet Yusuf to take him instead. They were so worried about facing their father without Benyameen.

Judaa decided he will not return to Canaan and will remain in Egypt until his little brother will be released.

The prophet was happy because he was testing the brothers. He is convinced that they all genuinely care for Benyameen. He also looked after Judaa when he remained in Egypt.

The remaining 9 brothers with heavy hearts made the long journey back home.

The father was waiting in front of his house awaiting their return. The brothers explained everything that happened at the palace.

When Prophet Yaqub heard the story of what happened at the palace he realised that Allah is putting him through another test. First with Prophet Yusuf and now with Benyameen.

He prayed to Allah to give him patience and to strengthen his faith.

At this point the prophet became blind because of his tears.

Upon their father's request, all the sons return to Egypt sometime later. They collected Judaa and once again faced Prophet Yusuf begging and pleading for the safe return of their little brother.

Convinced that all his brothers were sincere in their love for Benyameen the prophet revealed his identity.

Journeying with the Prophets

The brothers became very fearful and begged for Prophet Yusuf's forgiveness. The prophet told his brothers how forgiving and merciful Allah is and since they will be forgiven by the creator, he will forgive them too.

They all hugged and embraced each other. Given he was an important official in Egypt he could not leave with them but he sent one of his shirts to his father.

He instructed his brothers to throw this shirt on his father's face and he will regain his sight.

As the brother's camels were approaching Canaan, Prophet Yaqub came out of his room. He told everyone he could smell Prophet Yusuf in the air.

His daughters-in-law felt that the prophet will die in grief over Prophet Yusuf. They didn't believe him that he could sense the smell of his beloved son.

Finally, the brothers arrived home and again re-tell what happened at the palace. They placed Prophet Yusuf's shirt over his face.

PROPHET YAQUB CAN SEE AGAIN

The brothers were genuinely sorry for the way they treated their younger brother, Prophet Yusuf, and begged their father to seek forgiveness from Allah. Like Prophet Yusuf their father also told the brothers about the mercy of Allah and so long as they remain pious people Allah will forgive them and shower his mercies.

Prophet Yaqub and all of his sons went to Egypt. It was a very exciting time for the old prophet. He had longed for so many years to meet his son, and finally it was going to happen.

When Prophet Yusuf saw his father, he exploded with joy. He placed his father on the throne.

Then Prophet Yaqub and all of his eleven brothers bowed down to the Prophet Yusuf.

AND THAT WAS THE INTERPREATION OF THE DREAM HE HAD AS A CHILD.

The sun, the moon and eleven starts bowing down to the prophet.

And children, that's how the Bani Israel ended up in Egypt.

Nani Serena will continue telling her story to the Arshad grandchildren. The next story will be that of Prophet Musa.

SOURCE OF INFORMATION

From Surah Yusuf – Chapter 12

And to you there came Joseph in times gone by, with Clear Signs, but ye ceased not to doubt of the (Mission) for which he had come: At length, when he died, ye said: 'No apostle will Allah send after him.' thus doth Allah leave to stray such as transgress and live in doubt (verse 34 of Al-Mu'min)

TASFEER OF Ibn Kathir

CHAPTER 9

The Story of Prophet Musa Alayhi Asalam

The Arshad kids are bursting with excitement. Today is the day. Today Nani Serena will be telling the story of Prophet Musa.

"I want to know all about Prophet Musa because that's my name too", said Musa with the biggest of grins.

Aaron added:

"And my name is Aaron. Prophet Musa's brother is also called Aaron. Aaron is another name for Haroon".

"Yes children", that's right.

Before Nani began her story, she asked the children what they had learnt from the story of Prophet Yusuf.

Layla began her recap:

"Prophet Yusuf invited his father Prophet Yaqoob and his eleven brothers to live in Egypt. Prophet Yaqoob has another name. The angel sent from Allah gave him the name Israel".

"Well done Layla", Nani Serena praised her eldest grandchild.

So that's where Nani Serena began the story of Prophet Musa.

A very long time had passed and Egypt's population grew. There were the Egyptians and the Bani Israel, the descendants of Prophet Yaqoob (Israel).

The king of Egypt was a very evil king. He was called Firaun (Pharaoh). He disliked the Bani Israel intently and was very cruel to them. The Bani Israel had to work very hard with little or no pay.

One night when Firaun was asleep he had a dream. He saw huge balls of fire coming from the sky and all the houses of the Egyptians were burnt. The fire did not touch the houses of the Israelites.

The Firaun was very fearful of the dream. He did not know what it meant.

He summoned all the priests and magicians in the land to interpret his dream.

He was told that the dreamt meant there will be a baby born soon to the Israelites. This baby will grow up to destroy him and the Egyptians.

The Firaun was raging with anger upon hearing this interpretation. He commanded that all the male children born to the Israelite has to be killed from birth.

But there was a problem with that. If all the male children will be killed, then there will be no one to work in the land.

He then ordered that one year the children will be saved and the following year they will be killed.

Prophet Musa was born in the year that all the male children will be killed.

"But Prophet Musa was saved??" questioned a puzzled Musa.

With that Nani began to tell the extraordinary story of Prophet Musa.

Prophet Musa was the grandson of Levi who was the third son of Prophet Yaqub and his first wife Leyah. His father's name was Imran. His mother's name was not mentioned in Islam. He had an older brother Haroon. He was born in the year that the Israelites babies were spared and had an older sister Maryam.

Journeying with the Prophets ■ 67

The family were very frightened that their baby was going to be killed as he was born in the year that all the male babies were killed. But Allah is the best of planners and ordered his mom to place the newborn in a basket. This basket was then placed in the River Nile.

"What happened to the baby, Nani", enquired young Seth.

The basket floated downstream; Nani continued her story. The waves took it to where the Firaun's wife was bathing. She instantly fell in love with the baby. She was very different from Firuan. She was kind and merciful. She had no child of her own and suggested to her husband to adopt Baby Musa.

The Firaun thought it was an Egyptian baby and upon his wife's request they adopted Baby Musa.

So, children you see how we must always put our trust in Allah. He is the best of all planners.

Firaun wanted to kill all the Israelite babies and the one who will destroy him is the one he adopted.

"Subhanalla", all the children said in chorus.

Then there was another miracle.

Baby Musa was crying non-stop as he was hungry. But he will not drink the breast milk from any of the wet nurses in the palace.

Maryam, Musa's sister, advised that she knew someone who produces very sweet milk that no baby will refuse. She was referring to her own mum.

So Musa's mom was brought to the palace to feed the baby Musa.

"Indeed, such a miracle", said Aaron.

Prophet Musa grew up in the palace as a Prince. He was kind and Allah granted him knowledge and wisdom.

One day, he saw an Egyptian shoulder beating an Israelite worker mercilessly. The poor man begged the prophet to help him.

Prophet Musa asked the soldier to stop beating the poor man. But he continued and took no notice. He even started insulting the prophet.

Prophet Musa was a big and strong man and punched the soldier. He fell and died.

The prophet was very remorseful and knew that Shaitan has misled him in this action. Nani advised the children that whenever they get angry, they must seek protection from Allah because Shaitan will make them do bad things. The prophet heavily regretted his action and prayed to Allah for forgiveness.

The next day he saw the same Israelite fighting with an Egyptian. The prophet told him off and accused him of being a troublemaker. Upon which he blurted out if the prophet will kill him as he had done the previous day.

The Egyptian man upon hearing this news ran to tell the authorities of the prophet's actions.

The prophet was informed of this by a man who came running from the far end of the city. The penalty of killing an Egyptian was death.

PROPHET MUSA LEFT EYGPT

Fearful for his life, the prophet left the city in a hurry. He took no clothes, food, and even no means of transport. He bared the journey with just the shoes he was wearing.

He headed towards Midan. The heat in the desert was scorching. He walked such a long distance on the rough desert that his shoes wore away. He was now bare footed. He had no food or water. He was exhausted. But the Prophet did not despair. He knew that Allah would help him.

Prophet Musa finally saw a well. There were many men with their animals using the water. As the prophet took shade under a tree, he noticed two women with a flock of sheep, waiting to use the well.

He approached the women and asked about the men in the family as it was the responsibility of the men to water their flocks. The young women explained that their father was an old man and there were no other males in the family.

Prophet Musa helped the women and then drank enough water to quench his thirst.

At this point, the prophet had no energy left and prayed to Allah to help him.

And help was surely on the way.

As soon as he finished his prayer he saw the return of one of the women. She was there to inform him that her elderly father wanted to reward him for his efforts and invited the prophet to his home. The name of the old man was Shoaib.

They all sat together, and Prophet Musa told his story. They all listened intently. The elderly father reassured the prophet that he will be safe in Midan. He invited the prophet to live with him and look after his livestock.

Layla's hand went up:

"I need to ask a very important question. Was this Prophet Shoaib who called the bandits and robbers to islam".

"Yes, I want to know, because he also lived in the city of Midan", said Musa.

Nani replied that it could be but she doesn't know for sure and only Allah knows.

Since Prophet Musa was such a strong and honest person, Shoaib asked him to stay with the family and worked for him.

The prophet gladly accepted the offer.

Then one day Prophet Musa asked the elderly man to marry one of his daughters. He agreed on one condition. The prophet must live with them for eight or ten years. This he agreed to instantly. He was a fugitive, running away from Egypt and he knew Allah had answered his prayers. So, Prophet Musa married the older daughter Safura.

By this time Aaron could not contain his excitement.

"Nani", Aaron blurted, "Safura is your second name"

And indeed Nani's second name is Safura.

Prophet Musa toiled the land of Midan for 10 years.

Finally, his term of service was finished with his father-in-law.

The prophet missed his family and the land of Egypt very much and decided to make the journey back to his homeland.

By now Seth had a question of his own. He wanted to know if Prophet Musa had any children.

Nani answered his question by informing that Quran didn't give any information on that matter. She further mentioned that the bible state he has two sons, but Allah knows best.

MOSES RETURNED TO EGYPT

So, once more Prophet Musa is making the journey back to Egypt. It was a very long way back and after walking for a long time him and his family became lost. It was a very cold night and he instructed his family to stay where they were. He was hoping to get some firewood to warm his family.

He then saw a large fire. He walked towards it. The fire was by Mountain Tur. He then heard a very loud voice.

It was the voice of Allah. He was speaking to Prophet Musa. Allah told him to remove his shoes as he was standing on holy ground.

Prophet Musa was holding a stick in his hand. Allah asked him about his stick. He described it as his staff that he leans on and beat down branches for his sheep.

Allah then told Prophet Musa to throw the stick to the ground and when he did, it began to slither and shake. The stick had been transformed into a snake.

Journeying with the Prophets ■ 71

It was indeed a very large slithering snake. The prophet was so scared and was about to run away when the snake returned to his original staff.

Allah then instructed Moses to put his hand inside his cloak. When he withdrew his hand, it became shining white. It then returned to its natural state.

With these miracles the prophet made the journey to Egypt.

Prophet Musa's brother Haroon was also a prophet and had a vision of the task that Allah had set for him and his younger brother.

When Prophet Musa arrived, he found his older brother, Prophet Haroon waiting for him.

They are now going to confront Firaun to call him to islam and to liberate the Israelites.

PROPHET MUSA AND PROPHET HAROON CONFRONT FIRAUN

Prophet Musa spoke kindly to Firaun about Allah. He told him of Allah's mercies and that he is the one God, the only one to be worshipped.

Firaun reacted arrogantly and reminded the prophet of his past crime. He accused Prophet Musa of being ungrateful. He reminded him that he was raised amongst luxuries and wealth in his palace. Moses excused himself by saying he committed the crime of killing an innocent man in error and Allah forgave him.

Firaun really believed that he was powerful, and he is God. He commanded everyone to worship him.

Also, when asked to release the Israelites to him, Firaun refused saying that they were his slaves.

Prophet Musa decided it was time to show Firaun the miracles that Allah gave him. When he threw his staff down it became a serpent, slithering and sliding along the ground, and when he withdrew his hand from his cloak and it strongly shone bright and white.

Firaun was very dismissive of these signs and felt that it was just magic. At that time in Egypt, many people practiced magic. There were even schools that taught magic.

Firaun summoned all the best magicians in the country and set a contest between the prophet and the magicians.

The day of the contest was set. It was on a day when there was a large festival. Prophet Musa was very happy because in this way can call the people to worship one God instead of the Firaun.

The day arrived.

It was decided that the magicians will perform first. There were about 70 magicians all lined up in a row.

They threw their sticks and ropes. The ground looked like a sea of serpents, writhing and slithering. But it was just magic. It was not real, just an illusion.

Prophet Musa was very clam when he threw his stick.

Deep into the story the children were totally absorbed. Nani Serena asked the children if they had any questions. They had none. They were just eager to find out what happened next.

The prophet staff transformed into a huge serpent and ate all the illusionary serpents.

The crowd was cheering and clapping for Prophet Musa. The magicians knew then that the prophet was no magician, and everything was from Allah. They all fell in prostration declaring their belief in the Lord of Prophet Musa and Prophet Aaron.

Layla gave out a great sigh of relief.

The children were ready for their questions.

Layla wanted to know what happened to the magicians. The others wanted to know if Firaun and all the people believed in the one true God.

Another question was if the Israelites were released to Prophet Musa and his brother Prophet Haroon.

Rather than believing in the God of Prophet Musa, the Firaun was seething in anger. He sentenced all the magicians to death and their bodies were hung in the market Square to teach the people a lesson.

Firaun had everyone believed that he was God and now in front of everyone he was proven to be a liar.

But the evil Firaun came up with a plan. He called all his officials and informed them to spread the rumour that the prophet was helped secretly by magicians.

His anger by now reached no boundaries with the poor Israelites. Firuan instructed his guards to imprison and to even kill others some of the Israelites.

The Bani Israel started blaming Prophet Musa for their misfortunes.

Prophet Musa was powerless. But he never gave up hope. He knew that that the help of Allah will arrive.

There was one Israelite by the name of Qarun. He was a cousin of Prophet Musa. He was blessed with a lot of wealth, but he shunned his own people and join forces with the Egyptians.

He had so much wealth and riches that its keys would have been too heavy for even a group of strong men to carry, and the keys of his treasures were so many that they used to be carried on sixty mules! Many people wished they were wealthy like Qarun.

Firaun treated Qarun well and paid him a lot of money because he wanted to be kept informed about the Israelites. When people are mistreated for a long time there is a danger that they might rebel. Firaun felt that he will obtain inside information from Qarun if the Israelites were planning anything.

Qarun hated the poor people, and when Prophet Musa reminded him to pay zakkat to the poor he spread a rumour that the prophet instructions were only to make himself rich.

One day he gathered all his slaves to parade the streets displaying his wealth. Him and his horses were all clothed in gold.

But Allah caused the earth to swallow him and all his wealth.

"I guess no one wished they were Qarun now", said Layla.

"No, they didn't", responded Nani Serena.

Firaun summoned Prophet Musa to the palace. Him and his ministers wanted to kill the prophet. However, a relative of Firaun who a believer in secret objected.

Hence, Prophet Musa was set free.

THE PUNISHMENT OF ALLAH

Allah commanded Prophet Musa to warn Firaun to free the Israelites and to stop his torture and oppression. The prophet conveyed to Firaun if the oppression continued Allah will send his punishment.

Even so, Firaun ignored the commands of Allah and the punishment did come.

There was severe drought and all the crops died. The evil Firaun still did not obey the commands of Allah.

Then Allah sent a huge flood.

Firaun and his people began to take heed. They appealed to Prophet Musa to ask Allah to stop the punishment.

Allah did, and everything returned to normal except the conditions of the Israelites.

Hence, the punishment continued.

Allah sent a plague of locusts that swallowed up everything in their path.

Firaun and his ministers once again begged for help. Help came but the children in Israel were still enslaved.

Next Allah sent a plague of lice and then a plague of frogs. The people were terrified, and these creatures brought diseases.

Every time Allah's punishment came Prophet Musa asked Allah for relief, but the conditions of the Israelites remained the same.

Allah sent one final sign. He turned the water in the River Nile into blood.

Even after all the punishments and signs the Children of Israel were still enslaved.

THE CROSSING OF THE RED SEA AND THE DROWNING OF FIRAUN

A point has now reached when Allah stopped sending his mercies and favours and ordered Prophet Musa to lead the Children of Israel out of Egypt.

Firaun had an inkling of what was to come. He gathered his entire armed forces and prepare them.

This took all night and by that time Prophet Musa had already left with the children of Israel.

They had an entire night head start.

The prophet and the children of Israel had reached the edge of the Red Sea.

Nani's grandchildren were now on the edge of their seats bursting to speak.

"I feel like we are the Bani Israel being chased by Firaun and his army. I am praying to Allah that they do not catch up", said Layla.

Little Seth in a meek teary voice sad he will be very sad if they do.

Both Musa and Aaron that Allah will help them.

The Prophet and the children of Israel were trapped. At the back was the vengeful army approaching and in front were the turbulent waves of the Red Sea.

Fear and panic swept through the children of Israel. The prophet was at the back and could see the army approaching at a rapid speed.

But he reassured the people. He told them to have complete faith in Allah and they will be helped.

Prophet Musa called out to Allah who inspired him to strike the sea with his staff.

THE RED SEA PARTED!!!!!

Prophet Musa directed the Children of Israel to walk on the dry bed of the Red Sea to the other side.

They were in safety now, but the Israelites were still fearful because they felt Firaun and his army will cross the Red Sea too.

The prophet knew that Allah is the best of planners and they will be saved.

Firaun and his army rode fearlessly into the seabed, and alas!

The waves started closing in.

Firaun is surrounded by death on all sides. He knew then that his time on earth is up. As he was drowning, he repented to Allah and affirm his belief. But Allah did not accept his repentance. Firaun and his army drowned.

Prophet Musa, Prophet Haroon and the Bani Israel reached safely to the other side of the Red Sea.

Next time it will be the Yorkshire Lads' turn. Nani Serena will visit Omari and Zayn to continue the story of Prophet Musa and the Bani Israel.

SOURCES OF INFORMATION CAN BE FOUND IN CHAPTER 10

CHAPTER 10

Prophet Musa and the Bani Israel Settled on the Other Side of the Red Sea.

When Nani Serena arrived in Halifax Omari and Zayn were already at the window waving excitedly. They live far away from Nani and doesn't see her often.

This time they prepared samosas, chat, onion bajje and some iced soft drink. It was a welcome relief and Nani welcome her treats.

"Have you been catching up on the prophet stories"? asked Nani Serena.

"Yes", both children said in chorus.

"Shall I tell you what I have learnt", Omari asked Nani Serena with excitement.

Nani was happy to listen to her grandchild's understanding.

Omari began to relate:

"In the year prophet Musa was born the king was called Firaun, he killed all the male Israelite children. Prophet Musa was spared because Allah willed it, and Allah is the best of all planners. The prophet killed an Egyptian soldier by mistake and ran away to a place called Midan.

Now it was Zayn's turn:

"The prophet stopped with an elderly man named Shoaib. My daddy's name is also Shoaib. He married Shoaib's daughter Safura and remained ten years working for him. Allah ordered the prophet to save the Bani Israel and Allah split the Red sea so all the Children can cross over. When Firaun and his soldiers tried to cross they, all drowned".

"Masallah, well done children".

Nani started to tell the story of Prophet Musa and the Bani Israel's life in their new land.

The people on arrival were very thirsty. Allah inspired Prophet Musa to use his staff to strike a rock and twelve springs appeared.

Nani then asked the children a question.

"Why do think there was twelve springs"?

Omari's answer was that Prophet Yaqub (Israel) had twelve sons and the Bani Israel are all the descendants of the prophet.

Nani was amazed at the young Omari's recollections.

Indeed, all the Israelites are descendants of Prophet Yaqub whose other name is Israel. The twelve springs meant that all the tribes will all have their own springs.

The desert was very hot, and Allah sent clouds to the Israelites to shade from the heat of the scorching sun.

Prophet Musa also prayed to Allah to send food for them as everyone was hungry. Allah answered his prayers and sent special food called mannaa and quails from the sky. Indeed, Allah is great and merciful and can do all things.

"I guess the people are incredibly happy now. Allah saved them from slavery and gave them a new land, water and food", announced Omari.

Nani shook her head and continued her story.

Unfortunately, the people were not happy and kept complaining to Prophet Musa. They wanted onion and lentils like they had in Egypt. The prophet scolded them and told that they should be thanking Allah rather than complaining.

They then came across some people worshipping idols. They asked Prophet Musa if they can have some idols to worship. That was very ungrateful of the Bani Israel. Allah performed so much miracles for them and now instead of worshipping Allah, they wanted to worship idols. Prophet Musa reminded them of this.

Allah instructed the prophet to lead the people into the land of Canaan to help the oppressed people there. They refused saying that they had only just come out of oppression themselves. Who remembered the land of Canaan?

Up went Omari's hands.

Omari was very eager to speak what he knew about Canaan.

Journeying with the Prophets

"I remember Nani. It was where Prophet Yaqub had his dream on his way to Charan and on his return he built a mosque. In our days Canaan is now called Israel where there is Jerusalem and Palestine, and Allah promised this land to the Bani Israel", the young child recollected.

Indeed, Nani Serena was pleased with Omari's knowledge.

Nani continued to tell the children that despite Allah promising this land to the Bani Israel they were refusing to go and help the oppressed people who were living there.

Only two men were willing to go.

ALLAH'S PUNISHMENT TO THE BANI ISRAEL - LEFT WANDERING 40 YEARS IN THE DESERT

The Bani Israel's Days of Wandering began. They disobeyed the commands of Allah and now they are suffering the punishment.

Everyday was the same. They were walking aimlessly, with no destination in mind. Eventually they reached Mount Sinai.

There Allah commanded Prophet Musa to fast for 30 days. At the end of the 30 days he had to fast an extra ten days.

After the fast was completed, Prophet Musa was ready to once again communicate with Allah.

Forty days had passed since Prophet Musa left the Bani Israel. The Israelites were becoming restless. Among them was an evil man name Samiri. He began to lead the people astray. He told them that the prophet will not return, and they need another God. He asked the people to give him all the gold jewelry they brought from Egypt. He dug a hole in the ground and built a big fire, threw all the gold ornaments in, and then like a magician scattered some sand over it. He fashioned a golden calf from the melted gold. It was a hollow calf and made sounds when the wind passes through it.

Prophet Haroon was indeed very sad because these people have now become idolaters which is a very grave sin in Islam. But the poor prophet was helpless. The true believers distant themselves from this idol worshipping.

Whilst on the top of the mountains Allah gave Prophet Musa the ten Commandments in two tablets. These are the rules that the Bani Israel must follow.

When the prophet retuned to the people, he was furious, and his heart was filled with shame. The Idol worshippers were singing and dancing around their "living God", the golden cow Samiri made.

He tugged his brother, Prophet Haroon's beard, and questioned why he let this happened. But the prophet understood that his brother was helpless as they would have killed him if he had intervened.

Prophet Musa punished Samiri by sending him into exile to live the rest of his life.

The Prophet took 70 elders from the Bani Israel to Mount Sinai to repent to Allah.

They stood back whilst Prophet Musa went up to speak to Allah. When he retuned to the elders, instead of finding them in repentance they demanded to see Allah and only then they will follow him.

"They are indeed very ungrateful people, Allah had shown them so many miracles", Omari said in disgust.

"What happened to them"? enquired Zayn.

Nani Serena told the children that Allah caused the ground to shake and the Bani Israel were struck by a bolt of lightning that killed all of them.

Prophet Musa became very scared because these seventy elders were the best of people and now, they were all dead. He was fearful of facing the Bani Israel with such news.

Prophet Musa prayed to Allah and they were all brought back to life.

They returned to the people and Prophet Musa informed them about the Ten Commandments that he had received from Allah.

For many years, the Bani Israel wandered aimlessly in the desert. Prophet Musa endured a lot at the hands of these people.

When his Brother Prophet Haroon died, he lost his greatest supporter.

After many years Prophet Musa also died, and Yushra, took over the leadership of the Bani Israel.

Nani will be visiting the Mahmood grandchildren to tell the story of Yushra next.

SOURCES OF INFORMATION

Surah Al-Qasas - QURAN CHAPTER 28

So go ye both to him, and say, 'Verily we are apostles sent by thy Lord: Send forth, therefore, the Children of Israel with us, and afflict them not: with a Sign, indeed, have we come from thy Lord! and peace to all who follow guidance! (Ta Ha verse 47)

Verily it has been revealed to us that the Penalty (awaits) those who reject and turn away. (Ta Ha verse 48)

When this message was delivered), (Pharaoh) said: "Who, then, O Moses, is the Lord of you two?" (Ta Ha verse 49)

He said: "Our Lord is He Who gave to each (created) thing its form and nature, and further, gave (it) guidance. (Ta Ha verse 50)

(Pharaoh) said: "What then is the condition of previous generations? (Ta Ha verse 51)

He replied: "The knowledge of that is with my Lord, duly recorded: my Lord never errs, nor forgets, (Ta Ha verse 52)

Moses said to him: Woe to you! Forge not ye a lie against Allah, lest He destroy you (at once) utterly by chastisement: the forger must suffer frustration! (Ta Ha verse 61)

Throw that which is in thy right hand: Quickly will it swallow up that which they have faked what they have faked is but a magician's trick: and the magician thrives not, (no matter) where he goes. (Ta Ha verse 69)

So Moses returned to his people in a state of indignation and sorrow. He said: "O my people! did not your Lord make a handsome promise to you? Did then the promise seem to you long (in coming)? Or did ye desire that Wrath should descend from your Lord on you, and so ye broke your promise to me? (Ta Ha verse 86)

(Moses) said: "Get thee gone! but thy (punishment) in this life will be that thou wilt say, 'touch me not'; and moreover (for a future penalty) thou hast a promise that will not fail: Now look at thy god, of whom thou hast become a devoted worshipper: We will certainly (melt) it in a blazing fire and scatter it broadcast in the sea (Ta Ha verse 97)

28. He is the One that sends down rain (even) after (men) have given up all hope, and scatters His Mercy (far and wide). And He is the Protector, Worthy of all Praise. (Ash-Shu'ara', 28)

And among His Signs is the creation of the heavens and the earth, and the living creatures that He has scattered through them: and He has power to gather them together when He wills. (Ash-Shu'ara', 29)

Whatever misfortune happens to you, is because on the things your hands have wrought, and for many (of them) He grants forgiveness. (Ash-Shu'ara', 30)

Moses said to them: "Throw ye - that which ye are about to throw! (Ash-Shu'ara', 43)

So they threw their ropes and their rods, and said: "By the might of Pharaoh, it is we who will certainly win (Ash-Shu'ara', 44)

Then Moses threw his rod, when, behold, it straightway swallows up all the falsehoods which they fake! (Ash-Shu'ara', 45)

Then did the sorcerers fall down, prostrate in adoration (Ash-Shu'ara', 46)

Saying: "We believe in the Lord of the Worlds (Ash-Shu'ara', 47)

The Lord of Moses and Aaron (Ash-Shu'ara', 48)

Said (Pharaoh): "Believe ye in Him before I give you permission? surely he is your leader, who has taught you sorcery! but soon shall ye know! (Ash-Shu'ara', 49)

Be sure I will cut off your hands and your feet on opposite sides, and I will cause you all to die on the cross!" (Ash-Shu'ara', 50)

They said: "No matter! for us, we shall but return to our Lord! (Ash-Shu'ara', 51)

Only, our desire is that our Lord will forgive us our faults, that we may become foremost among the believers! (Ash-Shu'ara', 52)

Go thou to Pharaoh for he has indeed transgressed all bounds (An-Nazi'at:verse17)

And say to him, 'Wouldst thou that thou shouldst be purified (from sin)?- (An-Nazi'at:verse19)

Journeying with the Prophets

Moses said: "O Pharaoh! I am an apostle from the Lord of the worlds,- (Al-Araf:verse 104)

One for whom it is right to say nothing but truth about Allah. Now have I come unto you (people), from your Lord, with a clear (Sign): So let the Children of Israel depart along with me. (Al-Araf:verse 105)

When they had had their throw, Moses said: "What ye have brought is sorcery: Allah will surely make it of no effect: for Allah prospereth not the work of those who make mischief. (Yunus 81)

And Allah by His words doth prove and establish His truth, however much the sinners may hate it! (Yunus verse 82) 26.

Said Pharaoh: "Leave me to slay Moses; and let him call on his Lord! What I fear is lest he should change your religion, or lest he should cause mischief to appear in the land! (Al Ghafir verse 26)

Moses said: "I have indeed called upon my Lord and your Lord (for protection) from every arrogant one who believes not in the Day of Account! (Al-Ghafir verse 27)

A believer, a man from among the people of Pharaoh, who had concealed his faith, said: "Will ye slay a man because he says, 'My Lord is Allah.?- when he has indeed come to you with Clear (Signs) from your Lord? and if he be a liar, on him is (the sin of) his lie: but, if he is telling the Truth, then will fall on you something of the (calamity) of which he warns you: Truly Allah guides not one who transgresses and lies! (Al-Ghafir verse 28)

O my People! Yours is the dominion this day: Ye have the upper hand in the land: but who will help us from the Punishment of Allah, should it befall us?" Pharaoh said: "I but point out to you that which I see (myself); Nor do I guide you but to the Path of Right! (Al-Ghafir verse 29)

Remember Moses said to his people: "O my people! Call in remembrance the favour of Allah unto you, when He produced prophets among you, made you kings, and gave you what He had not given to any other among the peoples.(Al-Maidah Verse 20)

O my people! Enter the holy land which Allah hath assigned unto you, and turn not back ignominiously, for then will ye be overthrown, to your own ruin. (Al-Maidah Verse 21)

They said: "O Moses! In this land are a people of exceeding strength: Never shall we enter it until they leave it: if (once) they leave, then shall we enter. (Al-Maidah Verse 22)

(But) among (their) Allah.fearing men were two on whom Allah had bestowed His grace: They said: "Assault them at the (proper) Gate: when once ye are in, victory will be yours; But on Allah put your trust if ye have faith. (Al-Maidah Verse 23)

They said: "O Moses! while they remain there, never shall we be able to enter, to the end of time. Go thou, and thy Lord, and fight ye two, while we sit here (and watch). (Al-Maidah Verse 24)

He said: "O my Lord! I have power only over myself and my brother: so separate us from this rebellious people! (Al-Maidah Verse 25)

Allah said: "Therefore will the land be out of their reach for forty years: In distraction will they wander through the land: But sorrow thou not over these rebellious people. (Al-Maidah Verse 26)

Children of Israel! call to mind the (special) favour which I bestowed upon you, and that I preferred you to all other (for My Message).(Surah Al Baqarah verse 47)

Then guard yourselves against a day when one soul shall not avail another nor shall intercession be accepted for her, nor shall compensation be taken from her, nor shall anyone be helped (from outside). (Surah Al Baqarah verse 48)

And remember, We delivered you from the people of Pharaoh: They set you hard tasks and punishments, slaughtered your sons and let your women-folk live; therein was a tremendous trial from your Lord. (Surah Al Baqarah verse 49)

And remember We divided the sea for you and saved you and drowned Pharaoh's people within your very sight. (Surah Al Baqarah verse 50)

And remember We appointed forty nights for Moses, and in his absence ye took the calf (for worship), and ye did grievous wrong. (Surah Al Baqarah verse 51)

Even then We did forgive you; there was a chance for you to be grateful. (Surah Al Baqarah verse 52)

And remember We gave Moses the Scripture and the Criterion (Between right and wrong): There was a chance for you to be guided aright. (Surah Al Baqarah verse 53)

And remember Moses said to his people: "O my people! Ye have indeed wronged yourselves by your worship of the calf: So turn (in repentance) to your Maker, and slay yourselves (the wrong-doers); that will be better for you in the sight of your Maker." Then He turned towards you (in forgiveness): For He is Oft- Returning, Most Merciful. (Surah Al Baqarah verse 54)

And remember ye said: "O Moses! We shall never believe in thee until we see Allah manifestly," but ye were dazed with thunder and lighting even as ye looked on. (Surah Al Baqarah verse 55)

Then We raised you up after your death: Ye had the chance to be grateful. (Surah Al Baqarah verse 56)

And We gave you the shade of clouds and sent down to you Manna and quails, saying: "Eat of the good things We have provided for you:" (But they rebelled); to us they did no harm, but they harmed their own souls.(Surah Al Baqarah verse 57)

And remember We said: "Enter this town, and eat of the plenty therein as ye wish; but enter the gate with humility, in posture and in words, and We shall forgive you your faults and increase (the portion of) those who do good. (Surah Al Baqarah verse 58)

AND ISLAMIC SCHOLAR

Islamic scholar *Ibn Kathir*

CHAPTER 11

The Story of Prophets Yusha (Joshua) Hizqeel (Ezekiel) Uzair

As soon as Nani Serena arrived at the Mahmoods household the children were eager to do the recap of the previous story. They have been watching on Facetime Nani story-telling, so they will not miss out on anything. And today all the other grandchildren are listening virtually.

Keyaan was the first one to speak. Fixing his spectacles into position with some seriousness on his face he brilliantly tells his understanding of the Bani Israel on the other side of the Red Sea.

"Prophet Musa prayed to Allah for food and water for the Bani Israel. He struck a rock and twelve springs appeared. In that way all the twelve tribes could have their own spring. Allah also sent Manna and quails for them to eat. When it was hot, Allah shaded the Bani Israel with clouds".

With her hands up, Leyah was eager to tell what she had learnt:

"There was an evil man name Samiri. When the prophet went to speak to Allah on the top of Mountain Sinai, he asked everyone to bring their gold because he wanted to make a God for the people to worship. He said Prophet Musa was taking a long time because he was absent for 40 days".

By now Eva was bursting to speak and the words just keep flowing:

"Prophet Musa was very angry when he returned. He scolded his brother Prophet Haroon for not stopping the idol worshiping, but was okay when he knew that the Children of Israel would kill him if he intervened. The prophet chose 70 elderly men to repent to Allah on Mountain Sinai."

"Can I speak now", Siyana said. Her expression was one of relief that its her turn:

Journeying with the Prophets ■ 87

She continued:

"The Bani Israel were very ungrateful and instead of asking forgiveness from Allah, they asked if they could see Allah. Allah sent a bolt of lightening and all of them were killed. But when the prophet prayed to Allah they were all brought back to life".

"Can I also add that both Prophet Musa and his brother Haroon died by the end of the story and Prophet Yusha was put in charge of the Bani Israel", reported Keyaan.

Nani praised the children and introduce the story.

Nani Serena wanted to tell the children the story of three prophets. They were Prophet Yusha, Prophet Hiqzeel and Prophet Uzairs. Nani wanted to show the children the miracles Allah performed for these prophets.

Nani started this story by introducing who Yusha was in Islam.

Prophet Yusha was only mentioned once in the Quran in Surah Kalf. Muslims read Surah Kalf every Friday. All the other information about Yusha came from Prophet Muhammed (May Peace and Blessings of Allah be upon him). This can be found in Sahih Muslim and Sahih Bukhari.

Yusha was a student and a servant of Prophet Musa. He accompanied the prophet when he went in search of Kidr.

When Prophet Musa needed information about Palestine in Israel Yusra was one of the twelve men who was sent. They returned with news that the Palestinians were very big and strong. That was why the Bani Israel disobeyed Allah commands in the first place to go to Palestine to help the people.

But as the years went by the older generation of the Bani Israel died and was replaced by people who were eager to help the people in Palestine.

Palestine was a holy land where many prophets lived. When Prophet Yaqub and family left Palestine and move to Egypt, some non-Arabs people, with enormous strength took control of Palestine. They were very cruel to the inhabitants. They controlled everything. They did not believe in Allah and was causing a lot of corruption in Allah's holy land.

And that's why Allah ordered Prophet Yusra to lead his army to capture the city.

Prophet Yusha formed an army.

He did not let anyone join who was newly married, who had just built new homes, and those who had pregnant animals waiting to give birth. He wanted to ensure that his army would have no distractions.

They travelled for many days and finally reached the banks of river Jordan. They crossed the river and then arrived in the city of Jericho.

Prophet Yusra and his army were amazed at the beauty of Jericho with its huge beautiful buildings and tall strong people.

The battle started on a Friday and continued until the evening. As the sun started to set the prophet became very worried because soon it will be Saturday. Saturday was a holy day for the Bani Israel and they will not be allowed to fight. Prophet Yusra prayed to Allah to seek his help.

THEN THE MIRACLE

Allah stopped the sun from setting.

"Allah always help good people who pray to him", Keyaan said quietly.

"Yes Keyaan", that's true. It was a miracle and the sun remained in one place in the sky", informed Nani Serena.

Prophet Yusha and his men fought bravely and they won the battle.

Prophet Yusha died when he was a hundred years old in Palestine.

THE STORY OF PROPHET HIZQEEL

After the victory of the war the Israelites were now living in Palestine. It was during this time that a plague attacked the village. People started getting sick and were dying.

"Its like now Nani with the corona virus", said Leyah.

It certainly was. The people started fleeing from the Village. Allah was very angry because as muslims when there is a plague we must not leave and go to another place.

They travelled for many days and settled on top of a mountain. It was there that the angel of death appeared to them all and took all their lives.

"Oh no!, exclaimed Eva. "Did all the people that ran away really die"?

"Yes", they all died the same day" replied Nani Serena.

After a very long time a prophet called Prophet Hizqeel was passing and saw the skeletal remains of all these dead people.

He stood wondering over them, twisting his jaws and fingers. Allah then spoke to him and asked if he wanted Allah to show him how he can bring all these people back to life.

And of course he wanted to see this miracle.

A voice said to him:

"Call: 'O you bones, Allah commands you to gather up.'"

The bones began to fly one to the other until they became skeletons.

Then Allah revealed to him to say;

"Call: 'O you bones, Allah commands you to put on flesh and blood and the clothes in which they had died.'"

And a voice said: "Allah commands you to call the bodies to rise."

And they rose. When they returned to life they said: "Blessed are You, O Lord, and all praises is Yours."

THE STORY OF PROPHET UZAIRS

The miracle of this prophet is that Allah made him sleep for one hundred years.

One day prophet Uzair went for a walk with his donkey and took some food. After several hours of walking he came to a deserted place. It was a scorching hot day. He dismounted his donkey and sat under the shade of the Khaiba tree and ate his food.

He got up and saw the ruins of a city and the skeletal remains of people.

"It was just like Prophet Hiqzeel Nani, said Leyah.

"It was indeed like the story of Prophet Hiqzeel, but Allah will perform a different miracle here.

Upon looking at the bones, Prophet Uzairs wondered out of curiosity how would Allah bring these bones back to life.

Serena Husain Yates

Allah then sent the angel of death to take the prophet's life. And he lay dead for one hundred years.

And of course his donkey also died during this period.

Allah then brought the prophet and his donkey back to life. He now understood how Allah revives death when he realised, he himself had died for one hundred years.

"What did he do next"? questioned Eva. Did he travel back to his Home?"

And that exactly what the prophet did. When he arrived, everything was so different. He didn't know anyone. He rode his donkey to his house and still didn't recognise anyone. A hundred years is a very long time. Some people would have been dead, others a hundred years older and many more people were born.

He keeps introducing himself as Uzairs but everyone shook their head and said they didn't know him.

He then saw an old crippled blind woman sitting in front of his house. When he enquired whether the house was his, the old woman agreed. Prophet Uzairs came to realise that this old woman was his maid,

He introduced himself and told her how he had died for a hundred years and Allah brought him back to life. Although she recognised his voice she couldn't be sure.

She told him to cure her blindness and immobility, as the Prophet Uzairs used to supplicate to Allah to perform miracles.

This the prophet did. And she could see and walk again.

She was overjoyed and told everyone that the stranger was indeed Prophet Uzairs.

He took the prophet to meet his son who was 118 years old. There he saw many of his children and grandchildren. It was unbelievable what the maid was saying to them.

How could this young man be their father. They were very doubtful.

His son decided to settle the matter to see whether the stranger had a black mark between his shoulders. His father had one.

When the prophet showed him the mark, the entire family was overjoyed.

They told him that whilst he was away the evil king destroyed all the copies of the Torah, their holy book given to prophet Musa.

The prophet remembered that he had buried a copy and went to retrieve it. Unfortunately, it was damaged and could not be read.

The prophet, surrounded by all of his children sat under a tree and because he had memorised the Torah, he began to write a new copy.

Prophet Uzairs died after 40 years.

Nani Serena will be visiting the Yates grandchildren to tell the story of Prophet Shammil (Samuel), Prophet Talut (Saul), Prophet Dawood (David), Prophet Sulaiman (Solomon)

SOURCE OF INFORMATION

Oh! How will Allah ever bring it to life after its death?" (Al Baqarah 2:259)

And look at your donkey! Thus We have made of you a sign for the people. Look at the bones, how We bring them together and clothe them with flesh." When this was clearly shown to him he said: "I know now that Allah is able to do all things." (Al Baqarah 2:259)

We have made of you a sign for the people." (Al Baqarah 2:259

Did you (O Muhammad) not think of those who went forth from their homes in thousands, fearing death? Allah said to them, "Die." And then He restored them to life. Truly, Allah is full of Bounty to mankind, but most men think not. (Al Baqarah 2:243 Quran).)

AND LO! [In the course of his wanderings,] Moses said to his servant (fata), 'I shall not give up until I reach the junction of the two seas, even if I [have to] spend untold years [in my quest]! (Kalf:60)

TASFEER OF IBN KATHIR

SAHIH BUKHARI

SAHIH MUSLIM

Chapter 87 AL-A'LA VERSE 8

Chapter 92 AL-LAYL VERSE 7

SURAH TAWBA VERSE 30

TASFEER OF IBN KATHIR

SAHIH MUSLIM

SAHIH BUKHARI

CHAPTER 12

The Story of Prophet Sammil (AS) Samuel, Talut, (Samson), Jalut (Goliath) Prophet Dawood (AS) David

It was now the Yates Children's turn to listen to Nani's Story. As Nani Serena entered the room all hands were up in anticipation to relate what they have learnt from the last story.

Jasmine was the first one to speak.

"You told the Mahmood kids about three prophets and the miracles Allah performed to help them.

When Prophet Yusra was fighting the evil people in Jericho, Allah stopped the sun from setting. It was because the battle started on a Friday and the following day being a Saturday the Bani Israelites were not permitted to fight. So, Saturday only came when the Israelites won the battle.

Tariq added:

"Allah shown Prophet Hiqzeel how he can revive the skeletal remains of the people running away from the plague to humans again".

Amelia's Contribution:

"Allah caused Prophet Uzairs to die for one hundred years".

"These are all indeed great miracles", Nani said and praised the children for their good memory.

Today Nani is telling the story of Prophet Shammil.

As the years went by the Israelites started committing a lot of sins and even became idolaters. The ruler of the land was an evil king who mistreated them and shed their blood. They fought many battles. They will take their Ark of the Covenant to these wars because they believe it brought them luck.

"What's the Ark of the Covenant"? asked Jasmine

Nani replied that it was a chest containing relics from the time of the people of Prophet Musa.

They won every war they went to.

But alas!

They lost the war against the Philistines and their Ark was snatched from them.

When the king heard what happened he had a heart attack and died instantly.

The Israelites now were without a king and were like sheep without a shepherd. There was no one to rule the country.

It was then that Allah sent Prophet Shammil to guide the people of Israel

As time goes by, they requested that the prophet appoint a leader. They wanted to go into battle with the Philistines and win back their Ark.

One day Prophet Shammil prayed to Allah to help him choose a king. His prayers were answered, and Allah gave him signs of the chosen person.

There was a young boy name Talut, who lived far away with his father in a farm.

One day Talut and his servant were out looking for their missing donkeys. They spent several days looking without any luck. Eventually, Talut decided they must return home as his father will be worried about them and had no help in his farm.

However, his servant informed him that as Prophet Shammil lived in this land, they should pay him a visit and asked whether he can shed any light about the missing donkeys.

As they were walking they met a group of women who directed them to the prophet's house.

When they arrived, they saw a large gathering in front of the prophet's house. People had assembled there with the hope that they will be the chosen one for the leadership of Israel.

Talut greeted the prophet with much respect and asked about his missing donkeys. He was assured that all his donkeys were on their way home. Talut was relieved.

Prophet Shammil immediately recognised him as the chosen one.

The prophet told Talut there and then.

He is going to be the King of Israel.

The crowds protested at the Prophet's choice. They objected because they felt that Talut was a descendant of Benyameen and was very lowly without much wealth.

But the Prophet had made his choice informing everyone that it was by the will of Allah.

Talut's role will be to unite the Bani Israel and protect them from their enemies.

"Wow, Talut must have been very happy that he is now the king", said Jasmine.

Nani replied that Talut wasn't. He was worried about taking on such a big responsibility and felt he knew nothing about leadership and was just a poor shepherd.

But when Prophet Shammil told him that it was the will of Allah, he accepted the role.

King Talut started his duties.

An army was organised to fight the Philistines to win back their Ark of Covenant. He only chose those who were free from responsibilities. He did not accept anyone who was building homes, recently got married, and who was engaged in business affairs.

He prepared his army for battle by putting them through strenuous training. When he felt that they were ready he started putting his plan in action.

They travelled for many days and nights until they came to a stream. King Talut decided to test his army and commanded them only to drink amounts of water to quench their thirst.

Not all of them follow his instructions. Some were gulping down like there was no tomorrow. The king was very disappointed and dismissed the greedy ones from his army.

He needed his army to be sincere.

During the journey he put his army through many tests and by the time they reached the land of the Philistines, there were only 30 soldiers.

"Was Talut scared?" asked Tariq.

"No Tariq, he wasn't scared. He preferred an army of small believers rather than a large army of unreliable men", replied Nani Serena.

The Phillistines army was a large one. The soldiers were well equipped with their weapons. Their leader was a giantlike soldier name Jalut.

When faced with such a large army some of the Israelite soldiers ran away.

Rather than the whole army fighting, it was their custom to send one soldier from each side to fight with each other.

Hence, Talut asked his army who will volunteer for this position. No one did. They were all scared. He even offered his daughter's hand in marriage to the one who will fight Jalut. Yet no one volunteered.

Talut was very disappointed with his army.

But then a young boy from his army came forward and volunteered.

When the soldiers from the Philistines saw him, they roared with laughter. They thought it was a done deal that they will win the battle.

His name was Dawood and was from Bethlehem. His brothers were all soldiers and he was the youngest. He came to the battlefield to update his family of the news on the warfront. His father told him that he must not take part in any fighting.

Talut admired young Dawood's courage but felt that he was no match for the strong giantlike Jalut.

Indeed, Dawood was a very courageous young man and related that he had killed a lion and a tiger all by himself.

Talut was impressed and asked the soldiers to dress young Dawood in battle clothes and to give him a sword.

Dawood refused because he had a plan, a very good plan. He collected pebbles and put it in his pouch and took his slingshot out.

By now Talut was getting very worried and wondered how a few pebbles and a slingshot can help their victory against this huge army.

As he approached Jalut the roar of laughter from the opponent army grew louder and louder.

With a sword in his hand, Jalut was ready to cut off Dawood's head.

Dawood said to him:

"I face you in the name of Allah whose laws you have mocked, I am not scared of you. I believe in Allah".

With that he took a pebble, put it in his slingshot and hit Talut's head with extreme force. Blood was gushing out from his forehead. Talut fell dead to the ground.

The shocked army upon seeing the death of their leader ran away.

THE ISRALITIES HAD WON THE WAR

Their sufferings from the Philistines had finally come to an end.

Victory were theirs.

Dawood was a hero and the soldiers fetched him on their shoulders back to the palace.

King Talut kept his word and Dawood and his daughter were married.

Despite becoming the most famous man in Israel he remained humble.

He went to the desert to glorify Allah. Dawood was chosen to be a prophet of Allah.

And revealed the Zabour (Psalms) to him.

Allah also blessed Prophet Dawood to understand the language of the birds and animals.

There were many wars after and the prophet was victorious in all.

Eventually, Allah blessed Prophet Dawwod and his wife with a son.

His name was Prophet Sulaieman.

NANI WILL TELL THE STORY OF PROPHET ISA (JESUS) NEXT

Serena Husain Yates

SOURCES OF INFORMATION

246. Hast thou not Turned thy vision to the Chiefs of the Children of Israel after (the time of) Moses? they said to a prophet (That was) among them: "Appoint for us a king, that we May fight in the cause of Allah." He said: "Is it not possible, if ye were commanded to fight, that that ye will not fight?" They said: "How could we refuse to fight in the cause of Allah, seeing that we were turned out of our homes and our families?" but when they were commanded to fight, they turned back, except a small band among them. But Allah Has full knowledge of those who do wrong.

247. Their Prophet said to them: "(Allah) hath appointed Talut as king over you." They said: "How can he exercise authority over us when we are better fitted than he to exercise authority, and he is not even gifted, with wealth in abundance?" He said: "(Allah) hath Chosen him above you, and hath gifted him abundantly with knowledge and bodily prowess: Allah Granteth His authority to whom He pleaseth. Allah careth for all, and He knoweth all things."

248. And (further) their Prophet said to them: "A Sign of his authority is that there shall come to you the Ark of the covenant, with (an assurance) therein of security from your Lord, and the relics left by the family of Moses and the family of Aaron, carried by angels. In this is a symbol for you if ye indeed have faith."

249. When Talut set forth with the armies, he said: "(Allah) will test you at the stream: if any drinks of its water, He goes not with my army: Only those who taste not of it go with me: A mere sip out of the hand is excused." but they all drank of it, except a few. When they crossed the river,- He and the faithful ones with him,- they said: "This day We cannot cope with Goliath and his forces." but those who were convinced that they must meet Allah, said: "How oft, by Allah's will, Hath a small force vanquished a big one? Allah is with those who steadfastly persevere."

250. When they advanced to meet Goliath and his forces, they prayed: "Our Lord! Pour out constancy on us and make our steps firm: Help us against those that reject faith."

Journeying with the Prophets

251. By Allah's will they routed them; and David slew Goliath; and Allah gave him power and wisdom and taught him whatever (else) He willed. And did not Allah Check one set of people by means of another, the earth would indeed be full of mischief: But Allah is full of bounty to all the worlds.

(Al -Baqarah verses: 246 to 251)

AND ISLAMIC SCHOLAR

IBN KATHIR

CHAPTER 13

The Story of Maryam (Mary) and Prophet ISA (AS) Jesus

The Mahmoods' children have been long awaiting the story of Maryam and Baby Isa.

The day has finally arrived.

The children gathered around Nani Serena ready to give their summary of the previous day's story.

Siyana insisted to have her turn first. Siyana Safiyah is the youngest in the Mahmoods' household.

"I really like the stories you told yesterday, Nani. My favourite was Prophet Dawood using his slingshot to kill the Giant Jalut and the large army running away".

Leyah added:

"And my favourite was when Talut was searching for his missing donkeys and was chosen by Prophet Shammil to be the king of Israel.

"And what about you Keyaan"? Nani asked the eldest of the Mahmood's clan.

"I couldn't stop laughing when the evil king died of a heart attack when they lost the battle against the Pillistines", said keyaan.

Eva quietly said that the other children had already talked about her favourites, but she remembered that Talut's army only had 30 men.

Nani Serena was indeed very pleased that the children are enjoying and remembering her stories.

The story of Maryam started with her old parents Imran and Hannah. They longed for a child but weren't blessed with any.

Hannah was from the descendant of Prophet Dawood.

Hannah and her husband prayed to Allah and one day their wish was granted. Hannah was pregnant.

She was overjoyed and promised to dedicate her child for the service of Allah.

Just before the birth, tragedy struck. Hannah's husband Imran died.

When Maryam was born her mother was very surprised because she was expecting a son. She was now facing a difficult situation. She had vowed that her child will serve Allah but women were not allowed in the mosque without a guardian and her father had died.

The new mother turned to Zacharia for help. He was married to Hannah's sister Elizabeth. The Quran tells us that this family was from the house of Imran.

The suggestion was that a guardian will be appointed for Maryam to remain in the temple of Baitul Maqdis. This is now known as Masjid Aqsa.

"Who was Maryam's guardian at the temple"? Keyaan asked.

Nani Serena answered that question by telling an interesting event.

Many holy men wanted to be Maryam's guardian because her father Imran was such a pious respected person.

So, a competition was held. They all wrote their names on pens and threw in in the river. They had decided that the one that remained afloat will be selected.

Zacharia's pen did not sink.

Zacharia was the chosen one. He was selected to take care of young Maryam. He was very happy because he didn't have any children of his own.

When Maryam was old enough she went to live at Masjid Aqsa, dedicating her life to the services of Allah. Her uncle Zacharia, who was a carpenter, built a separate room for her in the temple.

Zacharia visited Maryam everyday and taught her about Allah. One day during one of his visits he saw out of season fruits in her room. When he enquired where they came from, Maryam said it was Allah who sent them to her. He was so surprised.

Some of the Bani Israel were becoming bad, not following Allah's laws. Zacharia prayed to Allah for a son to guide these people. His wish was fulfilled when a few days later his old wife became pregnant.

Six months after that a man appeared in front of Maryam. He was an angel. He came to give her some very surprising news.

"What was the news"? asked Leyah.

When Nani told her that Allah sent the angel to tell Maryam that she will give birth to a son, Leyah was very puzzled.

"But she is not married and she is a pious girl, how can that be"? enquired the child.

Nani Serena continued the story by telling the children that Maryam also asked those questions and they Angel reassured her it was by the will of Allah.

Allah can do all things. She reminded them that Prophet Adam and his wife were created without a mother or a father.

The angel told her that he will be a prophet and she must name him Isa and he will speak from the cradle. He will be a prophet for the Bani Israel and will perform many miracles.

When it was time for Maryam to give birth, she left Jerusalem and travelled towards the city of Bethlehem. It was a quiet area so no one will question her as to why she was having a child without a father.

THE BIRTH OF PROPHET ISA (JESUS AS)

Maryam had a normal pregnancy. The time has now come for the birth of the baby.

Allah guided her to a safe place. She sat on the trunk of a palm tree. Near to it was a running stream

It was here she went into labour. Her pains were excruciating.

Baby Isa made his entry into the world.

After the birth, Maryam was very hungry and thirsty. Allah inspired her to shake the date tree and eat the fruits and drink the water from the running stream.

He was a beautiful baby. But now Maryam has this dilemma to face. How will she explain his birth to the Bani Israel.

Allah sent an Angel to tell her not to worry. Maryam had full faith in Allah and took her baby to face the Bani Israel.

The people saw Maryam with her baby and started questioning her.

"What were they saying to her"? Eva wanted to know.

Nani Serena replied by telling the children some of the questions she was asked:

"What have you done"?

"You are from a good family, and your parents were pious."

"How could you have a baby without a husband"?

As Allah had directed her not to speak, she just pointed to her baby.

Then a miracle happened. The newborn baby began speaking.

He said that he was the servant of Allah and a Prophet. He told them that Allah sent him to guide the Bani Israel to the right path.

The people were dumbfounded listening to the words of this newborn baby.

Some were convinced there and then that Maryam was indeed a very pious girl and the Baby was a miracle from Allah.

But even after witnessing such a miracle there was others who believed that it was a trick that the Baby spoke.

As Prophet Isa grew his unique qualities and prophecies began to increase.

When Prophet Isa was twelve years old something interesting happened. Him and his mother were passing by a temple. There were many men entering the temple. The prophet decided to wander in with them leaving his mother outside.

He found himself in a room full of people listening to a lecture given by a priest.

The Prophet was very brave and stood up and started questioning him.

The priest did not know the answers and Prophet Isa continued asking questions.

Yet no one knew the answers.

Prophet Isa spent a long time in the temple and his mother went home with the belief that her son must have returned home.

When Maryam realised that the young prophet was not at home she quickly ran back to the city to look for him.

She found him in the temple sitting amongst the priests still debating.

As the prophet grew older, he began to study the Torah and follow the rules of the book strictly.

Nani reminded the children that Allah gave prophet Musa the Torah.

His knowledge took him to the realisation how the Bani Israel had misinterpreted and abused the words of Allah for their own benefits.

Prophet Isa's mission was to confirm the Torah, to make lawful things that were previously unlawful and to reaffirm the belief in One God.

Those priests were choosing their own law, making things lawful and unlawful as they wished.

They had violated the sabbath laws.

They ruled that the sick must not seek medical attention on the Sabbath day, there should be not eating nor drinking and people must not even plait their hairs. They made up so much different rules that contradicted the Torah.

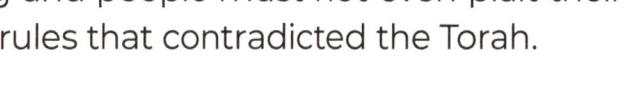

Prophet Isa broke all their rules when he fed the hungry people, made fires for the elderly to keep themselves warm, tend to the sick.

Prophet Isa was certainly not popular with the "so-called" higher priests in Israel.

The Prophet had profound knowledge of the Torah and was living by all its rules.

Allah also blessed the prophet with signs and miracles. Prophet Isa was provided with all the qualities from the one true God to guide and influence the Bani Israel.

One day Prophet Isa visited the temple and found more than twenty thousand priests. They all earn a living from the temple. There were more priests than visitors.

They charged the visitors lots of money to visit the temple. If the poor people had no money they will be turned away.

This day the prophet saw a huge flock of sheep waiting to be sold to the visitors for sacrifice. If the people want to bring their own animal to make their sacrifice, the priest will not allow it.

It was indeed not a particularly good time for the poor people.

It seemed that rather than worshipping Allah, the priests were worshipping money. The temple rather than a place of worship was more of a market and trading place.

The Bani Israel were indeed corrupted.

The temple was full of offerings whilst thousands living on the outside were starving.

Nani Serena noticed that Keyaan was in such deep concentration. Nani asked him to share his thoughts.

"I was wondering what happened to the son of that pious man Zacharia, he would be an adult by now"? queried Nani's oldest grandchild.

"Wow, Keyaan, thank you for listening so intently", said Nani Serena.

Nani informed the children that Prophet Zacharia's wife Elizabeth gave birth to a beautiful Baby boy. The prophet was ninety years old when his son was born. His name was Yahya, John in English.

Yahya was no ordinary son. Allah granted him Knowledge and wisdom. He was full of sympathy and compassion. He had full knowledge of the Torah and followed all the rules of Allah. He was righteous and free from sin.

Allah blessed Yahya with prophethood. He guided the people to follow the commands of Allah and refrained from committing sins.

Him and his cousin Prophet Isa lived in Israel at the same time, calling people to Islam.

One night both Prophet Yahya and his father Prophet Zacharia were killed by the rulers of the Kingdom.

PROPHET ISA BEGAN HIS CALL TO THE PEOPLE OF ISRAEL

Prophet Isa's struggle began. He began to spread the word of Allah,

and revealed to the people that he was a messenger from Allah.

When the prophet began calling his people to Allah's way, they asked him for miracles.

By the permission of Allah, he performed many miracles.

He made a figure of a bird from clay and breathed life into it.

At the time of Prophet Isa, the people were very advanced in the medical field, but even so they had not found a cure for blindness.

Prophet Isa was given the miracle of restoring sight to the blind, by the will of Allah.

He was also given the miracle of curing leprosy. The Bani Israel continued asking for more miracles. At one time they took the prophet to the graveyard and ask him to bring a man back from the dead. This he did.

Prophet Isa told the people that all the miracles were done by the will of Allah.

Even after these miracles, Bani Israel were still skeptical.

On another occasion, the prophet was passing by a graveyard when he noticed a woman crying over a grave. He asked her who had been buried there. The woman stated it was her daughter and swore she would not leave her because of her love for her. In her grief, she wished to die with her daughter, or her daughter be brought back to life. Prophet Isa proposed to her that if he brought her back to life again, would the woman then believe in his message. The woman agreed and the prophet proceeded to command three times that the dead girl rise from her grave. She was then was brought out of her grave.

Prophet Isa questioned the girl as to why it had taken so long for her to rise from her grave. She said that once she heard the first calling, Allah recreated her physical form. At his second command, an angel appeared over her head. Finally, her soul returned to her. As her soul returned to her body, the girl's hair turned to white from the horror that it might be the judgment day. The girl was appalled at the idea of experiencing the agony of death again and asked the prophet to return her to her grave. At this point, the mother is silent and astonished at what she saw. The prophet made dua to Allah to return the girl to her grave and to ease her plight. His prayer was granted.

Yet, they wanted to see more miracles.

They continued to bring him the sick, blind, and the infirmed. With Allah's permission, he was able to cure them all.

As the prophet continued to call the Bani Israel to follow the guidance of the Torah, the high priests were becoming more incensed.

One day, they brought a woman and accused her of adultery in front of everyone. The law of the Torah stated that those who commit adultery must be stoned.

They called Prophet Isa because they knew that he would oppose the stoning. In this way they thought they will demonstrate that he is going against the law of the Torah.

The prophet looked at the priests and was fully aware of all their evil deeds. He knew that they wanted him to go against the laws of Prophet Musa.

Prophet Isa smiled. He addressed everyone telling them that whosoever is sinless can stone the woman.

As they were all sinners no one dared to stone her.

That day, an important lesson was learnt.

Only Allah can judge.

As the prophet was walking away, he realised that he was being followed. It was the accused woman following him.

He questioned her without any receiving any reply. Instead, she produced a bottle of oil from her robe and mixed with her tears, she anointed the prophet's feet and then dried them with her hair. The prophet was very touched by her actions and prayed to Allah to forgive the woman's sins.

He continued to pray to Allah to show mercy and guide the people.

Prophet Isa had a group of followers, and they were called his disciples.

Once he told them, that he goes to bed with nothing and he wakes up with nothing, and yet he has more than everyone.

One day Prophet Isa was walking and saw a blind and crippled man. He stopped to have a conversation with him. The man said to him that although he is blind and crippled, Allah has protected him from the greatest trial which is disbelief.

The prophet touched the man on his shoulder and his disease was cured and made his face shone with beauty. The old man became one of his disciples.

THE FOOD SPREAD FROM THE SKY

A new Book was revealed from Allah to Prophet Isa. These revelations came to the prophet through Angel Jibreel (Gabriel), who is called *Ruuh al-quds* (the Holy Spirit) in the Quran.

All the revelations to the prophets came through Angel Jibreel.

Christians of today regard the Holy Spirit to be god, or rather, they hold that the Holy Spirit is one of the three persons in the One God. Whereas, Muslims believe that the Holy Spirit is Angel Gabriel.

One day Prophet Isa asked his supporters to fast for 30 days. They agreed and began their fast.

On the completion of the fast they followed the prophet to the desert. There were always many people who followed the prophet. Some were sick people hoping to be cured by the prophet.

But there were also a group of disbelievers who followed the prophet to mock and jeered at him.

Journeying with the Prophets   109

They had also fasted and asked the prophet to send something special from the sky to break their fast. There were thousands of people and they wanted the spread to be enough for the entire gathering. They saw this as an impossible task for the prophet and was convinced that he will not be able to deliver.

But they were wrong!!

Prophet Isa went in a quiet corner and prayed to Allah. His prayers were answered.

There was a table spread of food that descended from the sky. It was covered with a cloth. The prophet removed the cloth and saw the most mouthwatering food.

The people gasped in amazement. There were seven big fish, seven loaves of bread, seven bottles of vinegar, honey and an abundance of fruits. The beautiful aroma of the food filled the air. The people had never smelt anything so wonderful.

The prophet asked the disbelievers to eat first as they were the ones who asked for the food. But they refused and stated they will not touch the food until the prophet and his followers ate.

All the sick and infirmed people ate. Allah provided the people with another miracle. The sick people got cured.

The news of this miracle spread fast and thousands of people from the city came for this feast, and the food never ran out. This itself was another miracle.

After forty days, Allah directed the prophet that only the poor must be allowed to eat from the feast.

But this did not happen. The rich pretended to be poor and kept on feasting.

The poor was asked not to take away any of the food to be saved for the next day.

They did not listen either.

So, everyone disobeyed the prophet's commands.

"Wow, they all disobeyed the prophet's orders. Did Allah take away the food"? asked Siyana.

Siyana was right. The Table spread was lifted back to the sky where it came from.

Serena Husain Yates

This miracle remained in the people's minds for years and there were continued conversation about this miracle from Allah.

Alas! The priests wanted to kill prophet Isa. They were truly exposed for their evil deeds.

Prophet Isa was sitting in his house with his twelve disciples. He addressed them and said that one among them had betrayed him.

It was Judas who was the betrayer. He consulted with the head priest and asked what reward will be given to him if he delivered the Prophet to him.

He was promised thirty pieces of shekels. This was a lot of money in those days.

When this question was asked, he was so ashamed that he left the room.

Prophet Isa asked for one of his disciples to take his place as the soldiers were coming to arrest him. He told that person will be his companion in paradise. He asked that question three times and the same young man volunteered.

Allah changed his appearance to look like Prophet Isa.

Allah then raised Prophet Isa from a window from the corner of his house and raised him to heaven.

When the soldiers arrived, they took that young man instead and crucified him.

The disbelievers rejoiced. They believed that they had killed Prophet Isa, son of Maryam.

But the Prophet is very much alive today and living in the second heaven. Prophet Isa will return to earth before the Day of Judgement.

SURAH REFERENCES TO PROPHET ISA (AS)

2:87 We gave Jesus the son of Mary Clear (Signs) and strengthened him with the holy spirit.

2:136 We believe in Allah, and the revelation given to us, and to Abraham, Isma'il, Isaac, Jacob, and the Tribes, and that given to Moses and Jesus, and that given to (all) prophets from their Lord: We make no difference between one and another of them . . .

2:253 . . . To Jesus the son of Mary We gave clear (Signs), and strengthened him with the holy spirit.

3:45 O Mary! Allah giveth thee glad tidings of a Word from Him: his name will be Christ Jesus, the son of Mary, held in honour in this world and the Hereafter and of (the company of) those nearest to Allah.

3:46 "He shall speak to the people in childhood and in maturity. And he shall be (of the company) of the righteous."

3:48 And Allah will teach him the Book and Wisdom, the Law and the Gospel.

3:49 And (appoint him) a messenger to the Children of Israel, (with this message): "I have come to you, with a Sign from your Lord, in that I make for you out of clay, as it were, the figure of a bird, and breathe into it, and it becomes a bird by Allah›s leave: And I heal those born blind, and the lepers, and I quicken the dead, by Allah›s leave; and I declare to you what ye eat, and what ye store in your houses. Surely therein is a Sign for you if ye did believe."

3:50 (I have come to you), to attest the Law which was before me. And to make lawful to you part of what was (Before) forbidden to you; I have come to you with a Sign from your Lord. So fear Allah, and obey me.

3:52 When Jesus found Unbelief on their part He said: "Who will be My helpers to (the work of) Allah?"

3:55 Behold! Allah said: "O Jesus! I will take thee and raise thee to Myself and clear thee (of the falsehoods) of those who blaspheme; I will make those who follow thee superior to those who reject faith, to the Day of Resurrection: Then shall ye all return unto me, and I will judge between you of the matters wherein ye dispute."

3:59 The similitude of Jesus before Allah is as that of Adam . . .

3:84 . . . and in (the Books) given to Moses, Jesus, and the prophets, from their Lord.

4:157 That they said (in boast), "We killed Christ Jesus the son of Mary, the Messenger of Allah";-but they killed him not, nor crucified him, but so it was made to appear to them, and those who differ therein are full of doubts, with no (certain) knowledge, but only conjecture to follow, for of a surety they killed him not.

4:163 We have sent thee inspiration, as We sent it to Noah and the Messengers after him: we sent inspiration to Abraham, Isma'il, Isaac, Jacob and the Tribes, to Jesus, Job, Jonah, Aaron, and Solomon, and to David We gave the Psalms.

4:171 O People of the Book! Commit no excesses in your religion: Nor say of Allah aught but the truth. Christ Jesus the son of Mary was (no more than) a messenger of Allah, and His Word, which He bestowed on Mary, and a spirit proceeding from Him: so believe in Allah and His messengers. Say not "Trinity": desist: it will be better for you: for Allah is one Allah: Glory be to Him: (far exalted is He) above having a son. To Him belong all things in the heavens and on earth.

4:172 Christ disdaineth nor to serve and worship Allah . . .

5:17 In blasphemy indeed are those that say that Allah is Christ the son of Mary.

5:46 And in their footsteps We sent Jesus the son of Mary, confirming the Law that had come before him: We sent him the Gospel: therein was guidance and light, and confirmation of the Law that had come before him: a guidance and an admonition to those who fear Allah.

5:72 They do blaspheme who say: "Allah is Christ the son of Mary." But said Christ: "O Children of Israel! worship Allah, my Lord and your Lord." Whoever joins other gods with Allah,- Allah will forbid him the garden, and the Fire will be his abode.

5:75 Christ the son of Mary was no more than a messenger; many were the messengers that passed away before him. His mother was a woman of truth. They had both to eat their (daily) food.

5:78 Curses were pronounced on those among the Children of Israel who rejected Faith, by the tongue of David and of Jesus the son of Mary: because they disobeyed and persisted in excesses.

5:110 O Jesus the son of Mary! Recount My favour to thee and to thy mother. Behold! I strengthened thee with the holy spirit, so that thou didst speak to the people in childhood and in maturity. Behold! I taught thee the Book and Wisdom, the Law and the Gospel and behold! thou makest out of clay, as it were, the figure of a bird, by My leave, and thou breathest into it and it becometh a bird by My leave, and thou healest those born blind, and the lepers, by My leave. And behold! thou bringest forth the dead by My leave. And behold! I did restrain the Children of Israel from (violence to) thee when thou didst show them the clear Signs, and the unbelievers among them said: 'This is nothing but evident magic.'

5:112 Behold! the disciples, said: "O Jesus the son of Mary! can thy Lord send down to us a table set (with viands) from heaven?" Said Jesus: "Fear Allah, if ye have faith."

5:114 Said Jesus the son of Mary: "O Allah our Lord! Send us from heaven a table set (with viands), that there may be for us-for the first and the last of us-a solemn festival and a sign from thee; and provide for our sustenance, for thou art the best Sustainer (of our needs)."

5:116 Allah will say: "O Jesus the son of Mary! Didst thou say unto men, worship me and my mother as gods in derogation of Allah›?" He will say: "Glory to Thee! never could I say what I had no right (to say). Had I said such a thing, thou wouldst indeed have known it. Thou knowest what is in my heart . . ."

6:85 And Zakariya and John, and Jesus and Elias: all in the ranks of the righteous.

9:30 The Jews call ‹Uzair a son of Allah, and the Christians call Christ the son of Allah.

9:31 They take their priests and their anchorites to be their lords in derogation of Allah, and (they take as their Lord) Christ the son of Mary; yet they were commanded to worship but One Allah: there is no god but He. Praise and glory to Him: (Far is He) from having the partners they associate (with Him).

19:19 He said: "Nay, I am only a messenger from thy Lord, (to announce) to thee the gift of a holy son."

19:20 She said: "How shall I have a son, seeing that no man has touched me, and I am not unchaste?"

19:21 He said: "So (it will be): Thy Lord saith, ‹that is easy for Me: and (We wish) to appoint him as a Sign unto men and a Mercy from Us›: It is a matter (so) decreed."

19:22 So she conceived him, and she retired with him to a remote place.

19:27 At length she brought the (babe) to her people, carrying him (in her arms). They said: "O Mary! truly an amazing thing hast thou brought!"

19:30 He said: "I am indeed a servant of Allah: He hath given me revelation and made me a prophet."

19:31 "And He hath made me blessed wheresoever I be, and hath enjoined on me Prayer and Charity as long as I live."

19:32 "(He) hath made me kind to my mother, and not overbearing or miserable."

19:33 "So peace is on me the day I was born, the day that I die, and the day that I shall be raised up to life (again)!"

19:34 Such (was) Jesus the son of Mary: (it is) a statement of truth, about which they (vainly) dispute.

19:88 They say: "(Allah) Most Gracious has begotten a son!"

19:91 That they should invoke a son for (Allah) Most Gracious.

19:92 For it is not consonant with the majesty of (Allah) Most Gracious that He should beget a son.

21:91 And (remember) her who guarded her chastity: We breathed into her of Our spirit, and We made her and her son a sign for all peoples.

23:50 And We made the son of Mary and his mother as a Sign: We gave them both shelter on high ground, affording rest and security and furnished with springs.

33:7 And remember We took from the prophets their covenant: As (We did) from thee: from Noah, Abraham, Moses, and Jesus the son of Mary: We took from them a solemn covenant.

42:13 The same religion has He established for you as that which He enjoined on Noah-the which We have sent by inspiration to thee-and that which We enjoined on Abraham, Moses, and Jesus: Namely, that ye should remain steadfast in religion, and make no divisions therein: to those who worship other things than Allah, hard is the (way) to which thou callest them. Allah chooses to Himself those whom He pleases, and guides to Himself those who turn (to Him).

43:57 When (Jesus) the son of Mary is held up as an example, behold, thy people raise a clamour thereat (in ridicule)!

43:61 And (Jesus) shall be a Sign (for the coming of) the Hour (of Judgment): therefore have no doubt about the (Hour), but follow ye Me: this is a Straight Way.

43:63 When Jesus came with Clear Signs, he said: "Now have I come to you with Wisdom, and in order to make clear to you some of the (points) on which ye dispute: therefore fear Allah and obey me."

57:27 We sent after them Jesus the son of Mary, and bestowed on him the Gospel; and We ordained in the hearts of those who followed him Compassion and Mercy . . .

61:6 And remember, Jesus, the son of Mary, said: "O Children of Israel! I am the messenger of Allah (sent) to you, confirming the Law (which came) before me, and giving Glad Tidings of a Messenger to come after me, whose name shall be Ahmad." But when he came to them with Clear Signs, they said, "this is evident sorcery!"

61:14 O ye who believe! Be ye helpers of Allah: As said Jesus the son of Mary to the Disciples, "Who will be my helpers to (the work of) Allah?" Said the disciples, "We are Allah›s helpers!" then a portion of the Children of Israel believed, and a portion disbelieved: But We gave power to those who believed, against their enemies, and they became the ones that prevailed

IBN AL KATHIR

SOURCE OF INFORMATION FOR PROPHET ZACHARIA (AS)

(Al-An`am 6:85)

(Al-Anbiyaa' 21:89-90)

(Al Imran 3:38-41)

IBN AL KATHIR

SOURCE OF INFORMATION FOR PROPHET YAHYA (AS) JOHN

(Maryam 19:12)

(Maryam 19:13)

(Maryam 19:15)

(Al An'am 6:85]

(Al Imran 3:39])

IBN AL KATHIR

CHAPTER 14

The Story of Prophet Muhammed (AS)

Nani Serena is at the home of the Arshads' family listening to the children's recollections of the Story of Prophet Isa and his mother Maryam.

Layla started the discussion by giving her comprehension:

"Maryam's father's name was Imran. The third Surah of the Quran is called The Family of Imran and Prophets Zacharia, Isa, Yahya and Imran, all belong to the House of Imran. Imran was a very holy pious man but was not a prophet.

Maryam's mother's name was Hannah and her auntie was called Elizabeth. Elizabeth was married to Zacharia who was her guardian when she lived in the temple. Allah sent Angel Jibraeel to tell her about Baby Isa."

Musa carried on:

"Maryam gave birth to Baby Isa under a palm tree. She shook the tree and ate the ripe dates and drank the water from the stream. She was worried about what the Bani Israel will say about her because she had a baby and wasn't married. But Baby Isa spoke from birth and told the people that he was a miracle and was a prophet".

When it was Aaron's turn, Nani Serena was amazed how well he understood the story.

Aaron spoke of all the miracles the Prophet performed by the permission of Allah. He went into detail to recap how Prophet Isa breath life into the bird he made of clay, how he cured the blind, infirmed, those suffering from leprosy. He even remembered on the two occasions the prophet brought back the dead to life.

Nani noticed her youngest grandchild Seth sitting very quietly.

"Will you like to say anything Seth?", Nani spoke fondly to him.

She was quite taken back of how much young Seth remembered.

Journeying with the Prophets

"I remember how the people fasted for 30 days and asked Prophet Isa to send food from the sky. A table of food came down and thousands of people ate from it because Allah made the food everlasting. But when the people disobeyed Prophet Isa's orders Allah took back the table spread back to the heavens.

Judas, one of the prophet's disciples betrayed Prophet Isa to the high priests for 30 Shekels. When they came to kill the prophet, Allah made another disciple looked like the prophet. They crucified him instead of Prophet Isa who was taken up to heaven. He will return to earth before the Day of Judgement.".

Nani Serena started to tell the story of Prophet Muhammad (AS).

HIS EARLY LIFE

The holy prophet was born in Mecca in Arabia on 12 Rabi Al Awal. His mother's name was Amina and his father was called Abdullah and grandfather was Abu Mutalib.

All the prophets, but one, after the time of Prophet Ibraheem came from the lineage of Ishaaq. He was the son of Prophet Ibraheem and Sarah

But Allah decided that the last and final prophet will come from Bani Ishmael, the first child of Prophet Ibraheem and his second wife Hajrah.

Prophet Muhammed's father died before he was born.

At that time, it was customary for the children born in Mecca to be cared for by babysitters who lived by the hillside. It was a nicer, cleaner environment to raise kids.

The prophet's sitter was called Halimah.

Halimah loved the prophet very much and she brought him up with much love and care. One day when he was a young boy, something very strange happened. Two angels visited him, opened his chest, took his heart out and washed it with Zamzam water. They then put it back in its position.

"Goodness!" exclaimed Layla. "Did it hurt? Why did they do that?"

Nani told the children that the prophet felt no pain, and his heart was washed to prevent any influence from the Shaitaan. Prophet Isa and Maryam also by the permission of Allah could not be influenced by the Shaitaan.

Halimah was very scared and the prophet was retuned to his mother. Unfortunately, Amina passed away when Prophet Muhammed was just six years old.

Prophet Muhammed was now in the care of his grandfather Abu Mutalib. When he died two years later, the prophet's uncle, Abu Talib took charge of him.

The young prophet was a very happy child and accompanied his uncle on many of his journeys. On one visit when he was twelve years old, they went to a place called

Busra. They visited a monk called Bahira who saw some very special qualities in the young boy.

Hie exact words were:

"Return with this child and guard him against the Jews. A great career awaits your nephew".

Abu Talib was quite puzzled by the wise old monk's words and shrugged it off. He felt that his nephew was just an ordinary child.

The young prophet stood out from the people of Mecca. He had such impeccable qualities. He was pious, truthful, had good manners. There was no other child like him in Mecca. Everyone liked him and called him "Al Ameen". This means "The trustworthy".

His uncle although from a noble tribe was not wealthy, and the prophet helped him to take care of his flock of sheep.

The people at that time in Mecca were very ignorant. That period was referred to as the "period of Jahileyah", the period of ignorance. The people were very

Journeying with the Prophets

bad and didn't care very much for the laws of the land. As always, it was the wealthy ones who were the oppressors.

This grieved the prophet immensely.

One day, on a journey to Syria, he met a very wealthy widow called Khadija. She was a very noble and pious woman from a wealthy family. She was also a very smart businesswoman. She was a widow and many men wanted to marry her, but she refused all of them

She was so impressed by the prophet's honesty and knowledge and impeccable noble character that she offered him a job.

On his first business trip, he was accompanied by one of Khadija's servant. On their return, the wealthy widow wanted some feedback of the trip. What was related impressed her so much. He told her of the kindness of the prophet and the clouds that shaded them as they travelled the desert.

He went on to tell her of his good business dealings. He sold the goods that she gave him, and with the profits he bought other merchandise which he resold, doubling the profits.

She was so impressed by him, and although at 40, fifteen years older than him wanted to marry the prophet.

The next day she sent her sister to ask for his hand in marriage. The prophet was very surprised that such a wealthy woman with such beauty and nobility, the one who refused so many, wanted to marry him. He was only a poor shepherd.

Soon after the prophet and Khadija were married.

The prophet lived a very happy fulfilling life for many years.

When he was 35 years old something very momentous happened.

The Kabaah needed re building. All the tribes wanted to take charge of this job. It was a very difficult decision to choose.

One wise, old man stood up and said:

"You will listen to the first man that entered that gate", pointing to its direction.

The people agreed and patiently waited with eyes fixed at the gate.

The first one to enter was the prophet.

All the different tribes were consulting with him to secure the job of building the kabaah. After a while, the prophet came to a decision. He informed that a cloth should be placed under the stone and each tribe should carry it by holding a part of the cloth. Everyone agreed to this.

The result was that all the tribes participated in the rebuilding of the Kabaah.

It was at that time a person named Usman Ibn Hawairith arrived in Mecca.

He tried to tempt the people by using Byzantine gold so that they will become dependant on the Roman government.

Fortunately, his plan was foiled because the prophet intervened and warned the people of Mecca.

The prophet was very sympathetic to the poor and their needs, helping them as much as he can.

There was an instance when his uncle fell on hard times. Prophet Muhammed cleared all his debts for him.

Abu Talib had a son name Ali. The prophet took very good care of him and saw to all his needs, including his education. Ali went on later to marry the prophet's daughter Fatimah.

A year later, the prophet adopted another of his uncle's son Akil.

The prophet also had three sons of his own with Khadija and four daughters. Unfortunately, all his sons died in childhood.

THE STORY OF ZAYED

Zayed was a young child who was captured by some evil people from the arms of his mother. He was then sold as a slave in the market of Ukaz.

The child was bought by a relative of Khadija. Zayed was turned over to the kind Khadija who took the child home. He was brought up like a son in the family, rather than a slave. The prophet had a very special name for him "Al Habeeb", which means "my beloved".

He emulates the prophet and display his very good qualities.

At that time Musa's hand went up:

"I want to know what happen to the parents of Zayd. They must be very sad losing their child like this."

Musa was right. The parents of Zayd were very sad and mourned his loss. They prayed that the child will be returned to them.

Their prayers were answered. One day when they visited Mecca, they spotted their son playing near the Kabaah.

They rushed to him and offered the Prophet bags of gold to return their son.

The prophet refused the gold and told them of another way they can get their son back.

He suggested they call Zayd and let him decide what he wanted to do.

Zayd chose to remain with the prophet.

The father was astonished that his child chose to be a slave rather than returned home.

Zayd informed how well he was treated, the love and affection he received, of the beautiful qualities of the prophet.

On hearing this Prophet Muhammad's heart was filled with emotion and led the child to the centre of town and proclaimed him as his son.

THE PROPHET RECEIVED HIS FIRST REVELATIONS

When the Prophet was 40 years old, he used to escape his city to meditate in a cave on Mount Hira.

They were very barbaric people, addicted to superstition and idol worshiping in Mecca. They were always fighting with each other. He will sometimes spend the nights there as well, in deep concentration.

Then one day, the prophet experienced something amazing, but it also frightened him.

He was visited by Angel Jibraeel. He squeezed him and commanded the prophet to read. But he was an unlettered prophet and did not know how to read.

The angel squeeze him again and ordered him to read once more, but the prophet still could not read. On the third time the angel told him to repeat after him.

This was the first revelation. This surah is called Al Alaq and it's the 96 surah of the Quran. He repeated the following:

Journeying with the Prophets

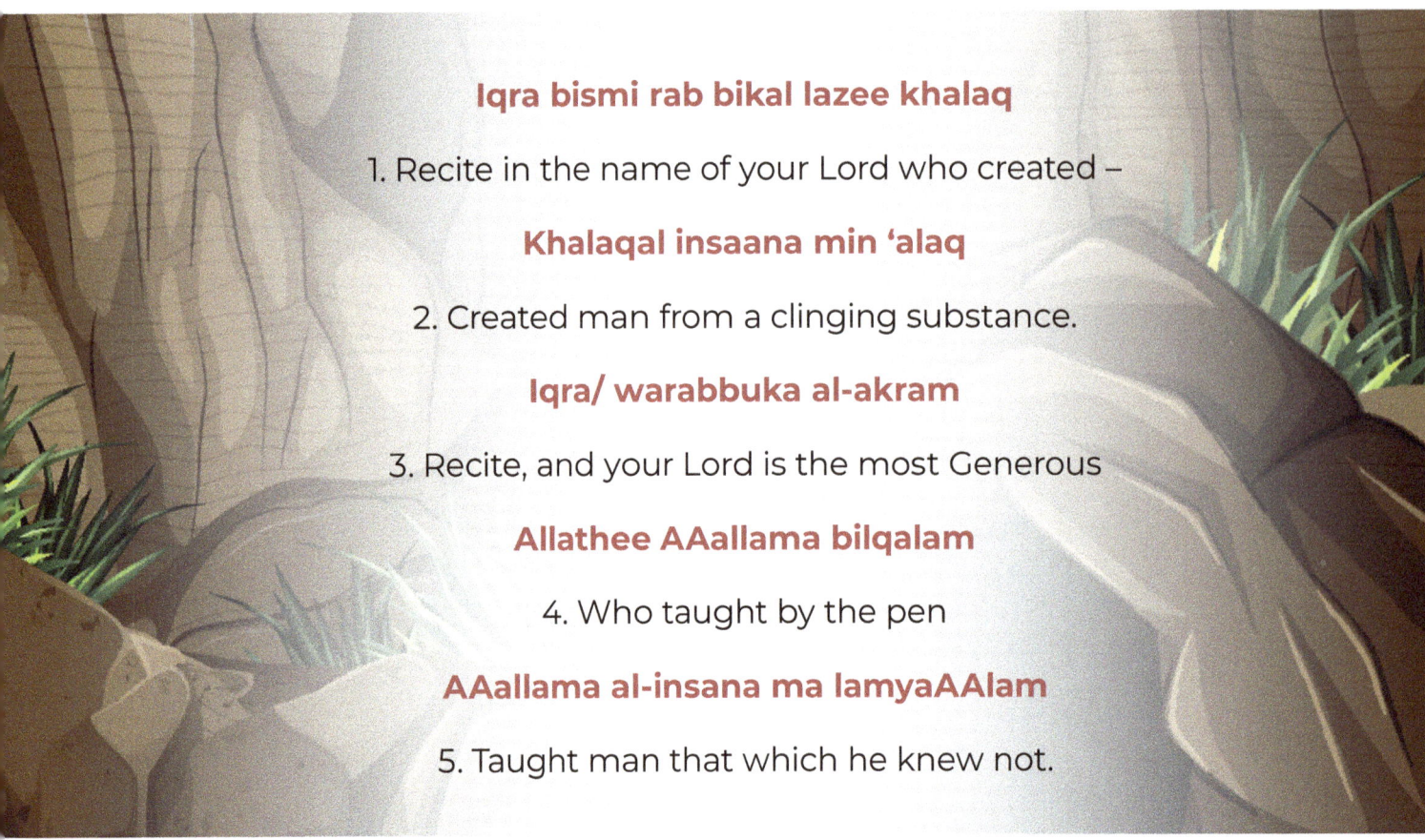

Iqra bismi rab bikal lazee khalaq

1. Recite in the name of your Lord who created –

Khalaqal insaana min 'alaq

2. Created man from a clinging substance.

Iqra/ warabbuka al-akram

3. Recite, and your Lord is the most Generous

Allathee AAallama bilqalam

4. Who taught by the pen

AAallama al-insana ma lamyaAAlam

5. Taught man that which he knew not.

The prophet repeated each word, trembling with fear.

He was still trembling when he arrived home much to the astonishment of his wife Khadija. He asked her to wrap him up. She wrapped him in a towel until he was trembling no more.

He felt that he was going mad, but his wife reassured him that Allah will not let such a thing happen to him.

Khadija went to consult with her cousin about the prophet's experience. He was old and blind and was well versed in the scriptures.

He cried out saying that the angel was the same holy spirit that came to Prophet Musa and went on to say that he will be a prophet to his people.

The prophet continued to receive revelations from from Allah. As these came down, he will ask his companions to write them down on sheepskin and then they will read them back to him, ensuring its written down correctly.

For the first three years the prophet only preached to close friends and family.

The first person to accept Islam was his wife Khadija, then Zayd, followed by his friend, Abu Bakr.

Then it was time to take Islam to the public.

THE PROPHET TOOK ISLAM TO THE PUBLIC

Nani asked the children if they had any questions before she continues. The children had no questions and were eager for her to continue the story.

Even after three years, the prophet only had 30 followers.

The people of Mecca at that time worshipped idols. The Kabaah was full of these.

When the prophet took his message public, he incurred the wrath of the tribal leaders who saw him as a great threat. Not only did he condemned idol worshipping, but he told that everyone is equal in the sight of Allah. Such preaching really challenged the local priests and tribal leaders. They were great oppressors of the poor.

They started plotting against him. They decided that each family should identify those followers of Islam and punish them in a tortuous way.

The people were beaten, flogged and thrown into prison.

The children gasped on hearing such cruelty. Layla wanted to know if they torture the prophet as well.

"The prophet was spared because he had the protection of his uncle Abu Talib", Nani told the children.

They tried to bribe him with lots of money to stop his preaching and join their religion. They offer to make him their chief and promised to consult with him on all matters. This message was conveyed by a messenger called Utba.

"What did the prophet say to him"? asked Aaron.

"The prophet responded by reciting the first thirteen verses of Surah Fussilat", Nani said.

1. *Ha-Mim.*

2. A revelation from Allah, the Most Beneficent, the Most Merciful.

3. A Book whereof the Verses are explained in detail; A Qur'an in Arabic for people who know.

4. Giving glad tidings [of Paradise to the one who believes in the Oneness of Allah (i.e. Islamic Monotheism) and fears Allah much (abstains from all kinds of sins and evil deeds) and loves Allah much (performing all kinds of good deeds which He has ordained)], and warning (of punishment in the Hell Fire to the one who disbelieves in the Oneness of Allah), but most of them turn away, so they listen not.

5. And they say: "Our hearts are under coverings (screened) from that to which you invite us, and in our ears is deafness, and between us and you is a screen, so work you (on your way); verily, we are working (on our way)."

6. Say (O Muhammad ﷺ): "I am only a human being like you. It is inspired in me that your *Ilah* (God) is One *Ilah* (God - Allah), therefore take Straight Path to Him (with true Faith Islamic Monotheism) and obedience to Him, and seek forgiveness of Him. And woe to *Al-Mushrikun* (the disbelievers in the Oneness of Allah, polytheists, idolaters, etc. - see V.2:105).

7. Those who give not the *Zakat* and they are disbelievers in the Hereafter.

8. Truly, those who believe (in the Oneness of Allah Islamic Monotheism, and in His Messenger Muhammad ﷺ) and do righteous good deeds, for them will be an endless reward that will never stop (i.e. Paradise).

9. Say (O Muhammad ﷺ): "Do you verily disbelieve in Him Who created the earth in two Days and you set up rivals (in worship) with Him? That is the Lord of the *'Alamin* (mankind, jinns and all that exists).

10. He placed therein (i.e. the earth) firm mountains from above it, and He blessed it, and measured therein its sustenance (for its dwellers) in four Days equal (i.e. all these four 'days' were equal in the length of time), for all those who ask (about its creation).

11. Then He *Istawa* (rose over) towards the heaven when it was smoke, and said to it and to the earth: "Come both of you willingly or unwillingly." They both said: "We come, willingly."

12. Then He completed and finished from their creation (as) seven heavens in two Days and He made in each heaven its affair. And We adorned the nearest (lowest) heaven with lamps (stars) to be an adornment as well as to guard (from the devils by using them as missiles against the devils). Such is the Decree of Him the All-Mighty, the All-Knower.

13. But if they turn away, then say (O Muhammad ﷺ): "I have warned you of a *Sa'iqah* (a destructive awful cry, torment, hit, a thunderbolt) like the *Sa'iqah* which overtook 'Ad and Thamud (people)."

The prophet then related to him about what had happened to the people of Aad and Thamud.

Such was the prophet's reply to Utba's proposition.

When this plan failed, they approached Abu Talib to ask his nephew to stop preaching islam to the people.

The prophet gave this beautiful response to his uncle:

"If they were to put the sun in my right hand and the moon in my left to stop preaching Islam, I will never stop."

Abu Talib loved the prophet very much and told him to continue preaching and he will never desert him.

THE FIRST HIJRAH (MIGRATION)

Despite the torture and oppression, many people were joining the religion of Islam.

At that time there was a very kind Christian king, Al Najashi, ruling Abyssinia. When the persecution became unbearable, the prophet advised them to emigrate to Abyssinia. This country is now called Ethiopia.

To avoid detection, only fifteen families migrated initially. This was called the first Hijrah in islam and happened in the fifth year of the prophet's mission.

They were received very kindly and others followed later. The number of migrants soon reached 100.

The leaders in Mecca eventually realized what was happening and they were furious and decided to act.

They sent two delegates to the king and requested that all migrants be returned to Mecca.

The king decided to hold a court and the fugitives were summoned.

Their spokespersons were Jabbar and Ali, sons of Abu Talib.

They explained the conditions they were living in because they refused to worship idols and believed in one God. They told him about the Prophet and his message.

They spoke very well pleading their cause to the king.

He was very sympathetic and asked the delegates to retun to their land and not to interfere with the migrants.

The prophet continued receiving revelations from Allah and continued to spread the message of Islam.

The people started asking him for signs from Allah. He responded by telling that Allah had not sent him to perform miracles but to preach islam.

He told them that all the prophets came with various miracles and yet the people returned to disbelief.

The quran tells us in seventeen places where the prophet was challenged to show signs and each time he gave the same answer.

Nothing seemed to be working, and Abu Talib was approached again to abandon his nephew. But although a non-believer himself, he stood by his nephew.

THE STORY OF HOW Umar ibn Al Khattab became Muslim

Umar belong to the Qureshi tribe and was a great oppressor of Islam. He was a very influential person in his tribe and the prophet prayed that he would accept the message of Islam.

One day he went fully armed looking for the prophet. He wanted to kill him. As he was approaching Mount Safa, where the prophet and his followers were assembled, he was stop by one of his tribesman, Nu'aym Ibn 'Abdullah. Nu'aym noticed his sword hanging from his neck and his aggressiveness. So, he asked him where he was going. His response was:

"I seek for Muhammad," was 'Umar's reply, *"And I will slay him; he has forsaken our religion, shattered the unity of the Quraysh; ridiculed them and vilified their gods. Today I will settle the matter once and for all."*

Nu'aym himself had secretly embraced Islam and informed Omar that his own sister Fatima bint al-Khattab and her husband, Sa'id Ibn Zayd, were also muslims. Seething with anger, Umar made a detour to confront the couple.

Umar immediately hurried on to the house of his sister. On approach he could hear the recitation of Surah Ta Ha (20th Chapter of the Qur'an) When Fatima heard the footsteps of her brother, she quickly hid the manuscript.

But he had already heard the recitation and demanded:

"What was this nonsense murmur that I heard? I know that both of you have joined the sect of Muhammad.

With these words, Umar threw himself upon his brother-in-law. Fatima rushed in to save her husband, but Umar struck her hard and wounded her.

The brave couple were not afraid and confronted Umar by asserting:

"Yes, we are Muslims; we believed in Allah and His Prophet (sallallahu 'alayhi wa sallam); do whatever you will."

Umar felt so ashamed of his actions when he saw the blood pouring out of his sister's mouth and asked them to show him the manuscript of Surah Taha.

Fatima replied that only the pure can touch these words of Allah and he was impure from polytheism.

Umar took a bath, and after reading just a few lines, he exclaimed in amazement:

"How noble and sublime is this speech!"

Umar left his sister's house and rushed to the prophet. The prophet and the followers thought he had come to hurt them.

The prophet very respectfully asked the purpose of his visit, to which he replied:

"I have come to declare that I believe in one God and you are his messenger".

Umar has now become a follower of Islam.

Umar proclaimed his faith publicly and his reversion had a miraculous effect on the people of Makkah.

The number of followers of Islam grew and so was the hatred of the non-believers.

The leaders imposed a total ban on contact with the prophet's family. They had to leave Mecca. During this period the prophet and his companions remained indoors resulting in the lack of progress of islam.

The ban on the prophet's family was lifted after three years and he returned to Mecca.

The following year was a very sad year for the prophet. He lost both his wife Khadija and Uncle Abu Tablib.

The children had been quiet for quite awhile, until Layla spoke.

"I am so worried now for the prophet because his uncle protected him from the enemies and his wife supported him in all of his mission."

It was indeed a very difficult time for the prophet.

It was reported that he said of this time, "Quraysh never harmed me so much as after the death of Abu Talib."

Whenever he saw his daughter, Fatima, cry at the insults and harm he endured, he would tell her, "Do not cry, O Fatima! Your father has Allah for his protector."

There was a very pious woman named Sawda who had emigrated with her husband to Abyssinia during the first Hijrah. When her husband died, she returned to Mecca. She sought shelter with the prophet. The prophet recognised the sacrifices Sawda made for Islam and ended up marrying her.

THE PROPHET'S ACCENSION TO HEAVEN

Nani Serena ensured she has all the children's attention because she wanted to tell them about this marvelous journey that the prophet made.

It was in the night. The prophet was fast asleep when Angel Jibreel paid him a visit. He was going to prepare him to make a very important journey in his life. He opened his chest and washed his heart with Zam Zam water. He then emptied a vessel made of gold containing wisdom and faith into the Prophet's heart. This is to prepare him for the journey. To make this journey he bought a beautiful horse with wings. His name is Buraq. Jibreel offered the prophet two cups from which to drink, one containing milk and the other containing wine. The Prophet chooses to drink the milk instead of the wine.

Jibreel told him, "Praise be to Allah Who guided you to the fitrah (right path)"

The Buraq carries the Prophet to the Al-Aqsa Mosque in Jerusalem

The first part of the journey is called Isra.

At Masjid Al Aqsa he finds three very important prophets. Prophets Ibraheem, Musa and Isa.(Peace and blessings be upon them all).

The prophet led them in salah there.

The next part of the journey is marked by Prophet Muhammad's ascension to the heavens. Here, all the laws of nature and the concepts of time and space as we know cease to apply and everything the Prophet experiences and sees is beyond human comprehension. At each of the seven heavens, the Prophet accompanied by Jibreel, encounters a gate and a watcher. At the gate of the lowest heaven, Jibreel asks the gate-keeper to open the gate.

The gate-keeper asks, "Who is it?"

"It is Jibreel," he answers.

The gate-keeper says, "Who is accompanying you?"

Jibreel says, "It is Muhammad."

The gate-keeper then says, "Has he been called?"

Jibreel says, "Yes."

The gate-keeper says, "He is welcomed. What a wonderful visit this is!"

The prophet proceeded to visit all seven levels of heaven and the same questions were asked and the same answers given.

At every heaven, he met with a prophet.

In the first heaven he encountered Prophet Adam who greeted him with delight.

The prophet gave him his salaams and the reply was:

"Welcome my son, welcome O Prophet of Allah!"

In the second heaven he met Prophets Isa and Yahya, Yusuf in the third heaven; Idris in the fourth heaven; Harun in the fifth heaven; Musa in the sixth heaven; and finally Ibrahim, the father of prophets in the seventh heaven.

"What an absolutely remarkable journey", exclaimed Layla.

Taking a deep breath Musa spoke:

"This journey indeed is beyond human comprehension".

During this journey he is shown the Bayt al-Ma'moor (the qiblah of the angels) that sits above the Kabaah, and scenes can be viewed from paradise and hell.

In the next dimension through the seventh heaven the prophet saw the Sidrat al-Muntaha (the Lote-tree) whose fruits are as big as jugs and its leaves as big as elephant ears. Here, Jibreel asks the prophet to proceed alone. No one from among Allah's creation has ever gone beyond Sidrat al-Muntaha.

Journeying with the Prophets

Here he had a conversation with Allah.

"Did he actually see Allah"? asked Aaron.

Nani replied that no one has never seen Allah but the prophet converse with him from a distance.

During this meeting. Allah informed the prophet that his ummah must pray 50 times per day.

On descending, the prophet told Prophet Musa about this. He suggested to the prophet to return to Allah and ask for less. This the prophet did twice and finally he was told that we must pray five times a day and will receive the reward of 50.

"SubhanAllah" said Seth. "Indeed, Allah is so merciful".

This remarkable journey has now ended, and the prophet is on his way back to earth.

On his descent he saw a Caravan en- route heading towards Mecca, with a lost camel that the traders were looking for.

The prophet informed everyone of his remarkable journey. The disbelievers ridicule him and accused him of lying.

As the prophet had never visited Masjid Al-Aqsa he was asked for its description. He gave a very detailed description. He also described the caravan he saw en route, and even when this was proven to be accurate, the disbelieve continued. They even accused the prophet of insanity.

Islam started spreading rapidly after this, much to the fury of the disbelievers. They made their mind up that the prophet should be killed.

Their plan was that one man will be chosen from each of their tribes, and they will attack the prophet simultaneously.

But Allah sent an Angel to inform the prophet and told him leave Mecca for Medina. This he did with his trusted companion Abu Bakar.

They went south of Mecca to the Mountain cave of Thawr and then travelled north to Medina.

They foiled all attempts from the disbelievers and arrived safely in Medina.

The people gave a warm welcome to the prophet and his companions. The people living in Mecca also gradually made that move to Medina.

The prophet settled in Medina and made it a state. He continued to receive revelations form Allah to guide the people how to live. Islam started spreading fast to the neighboring lands, and many rulers and their countries accepted Islam.

Today, Islam is the second largest religion in the world with the prediction that it will be the largest by the Year 2070.

SOURCES OF INFORMATION

The Seerah of the Prophet Muhammed (May peace and blessings of Allah be upon him)

Hadiths:

Sahih Muslim

Sahih Bukari